HENRY KECK STAINED GLASS STUDIO, 1913–1974

A York State Book

Figure 1. Henry Keck in 1939. Photo, Keck Archives.

HENRY KECK
STAINED GLASS STUDIO
1913–1974

Edited by
CLEOTA REED

SYRACUSE UNIVERSITY PRESS   1985

Copyright © 1985 by SYRACUSE UNIVERSITY PRESS
Syracuse, New York 13210

First Edition

This book was sponsored by the Institute for the Development of Evolutive Architecture (IDEA), Inc., Syracuse, New York, and its preparation was made possible in part by grants of public funds from the New York State Council on the Arts and the New York Council for the Humanities.

Library of Congress Cataloging in Publication Data
Main entry under title:

Henry Keck Stained Glass Studio, 1913–1974.

  (A York State book)
  Bibliography: p.
  Includes index.
  1. Henry Keck Stained Glass Studio. 2. Glass painting and staining—New York (State)—Syracuse—History—20th century. I. Reed, Cleota.
NK5398.H46H46 1985   748.59147′66   85-2593
ISBN 0-8156-2328-3
ISBN 0-8156-0194-8 (pbk.)

Manufactured in the United States of America

This book is dedicated to
two master stained glass artists
of the twentieth century—
HENRY KECK
and
STANLEY ELMORE WORDEN

We acknowledge with deep gratitude financial support for publication
generously provided by

Bristol-*Syracuse*
Mr. and Mrs. Sherwood Finn
Lauren Ginsburg
The Tarky Lombardi Family
Mr. and Mrs. Richard C. Pietrafesa

THE PUBLISHER

Contents

Color Plates

Contributors

COY L. LUDWIG is Associate Professor of Art and Director of Tyler Art Gallery, State University College at Oswego, New York. He is the author of *Maxfield Parrish* (1973) and numerous articles and exhibition catalogues. His *The Arts and Crafts Movement in New York State (1890s–1920s)* (Hamilton, N.Y.: Gallery Association of New York State, 1983) accompanied a traveling exhibition which he organized and which included works from the Keck Studio.

CLEOTA REED is a ceramist and historian of the American Arts and Crafts Movement. She is the author of studies of the architect Ward Wellington Ward, the historian and critic Irene Sargent, and the ceramist Henry Chapman Mercer. She has been curator of major exhibitions of the work of Ward Wellington Ward and of the Henry Keck Studio.

DOROTHY FRANCES TERINO holds graduate degrees in Information Studies and Fine Arts from Syracuse University. Her M.A. thesis in Fine Arts was a history of the Keck Studio. She was chief research associate with Cleota Reed for a study of the Keck Archives and also for the Ward Wellington Ward research project.

HELEN JACKSON ZAKIN is Associate Professor of Art at State University College at Oswego, New York. She is a scholar of medieval and American stained glass and has published and lectured widely. Since 1981 she has been a member of the Board of Governors and Regional Director of the Census of Stained Glass in America.

Preface

LTHOUGH STAINED GLASS has been an important part of the built environment of American cities, towns, and villages for well over a century, it has received remarkably little scholarly attention compared to the other fine and decorative arts of the United States. Studies have appeared of a few major figures—Louis Comfort Tiffany and John La Farge, especially—but the many regional studios located outside the big cities have been almost entirely neglected. This is regrettable, since the best of them created windows that rank among the finest work in the medium nationwide. The present study of the Henry Keck Studio is the first book-length examination of an American regional stained glass studio—a studio that maintained an exceptionally high level of work from its founding in 1913 to its closing in 1974.

The publication of this book is an outgrowth of a major exhibition of the work of the Henry Keck Stained Glass Studio, held at the Onondaga Historical Museum in Syracuse, New York, October 15, 1983, to February 1, 1984. It also marks the transfer of the Keck Studio Archives to the Onondaga Historical Association in Syracuse. It is the product of research begun intensively in 1978 under the sponsorship of the Institute for the Development of Evolutive Architecture (IDEA), Inc., in Syracuse. An organization of scholars in the fields of architecture, art and architectural history, solar energy, education, information studies, historic preservation, and community development who are committed to fostering the study of the arts, crafts, and technology of America's built environment, IDEA reaches the public through exhibitions, publications, media presentations, reports on historic documentation, seminars, and other programs of professional quality.

An early IDEA project, resulting in a traveling exhibition and catalogue of the work of the Syracuse architect Ward Wellington Ward, drew attention to many of the Keck Studio stained glass installations in Ward houses in upstate New York. Supported by a grant from the New York State Council on the Arts, in 1978 IDEA began to catalogue the Studio's archives, a rare and wonderful collection of drawings and business records documenting every aspect of the life of the Studio. Over the next four years, Dorothy Terino, Stanley Worden, and I spent countless hours labeling drawings, reading ledgers and order books, unrolling and studying cartoons, and in every way possible documenting the Studio's work. I examined and photographed installations, large and small, throughout New York State and elsewhere. Dorothy Terino analyzed the Studio's records and unearthed information from many other sources to document her history of the Studio and its work. This teamwork has produced what may be the most complete and thoroughly documented record of the work of an American regional stained glass studio.

In 1982, funded in part by the New York Council for the Humanities, IDEA produced an interpretive videotape for public broadcast "Reflections of a Stained Glass Artist: Stanley Worden and the Keck Studio." This videotape also accompanied the Keck Studio exhibition. In it, Stanley Worden, who joined the Studio as an apprentice, became its head designer, and succeeded Henry Keck as director, explains and demonstrates important aspects of the art and craft of stained glass. Gail Wiltshire and Joseph Hoffman produced the tape.

Many hands generously contributed to the success of all these efforts. Without Stanley Worden the original high hopes of the investigators would never have been realized. This book is a testimonial to his limitless resourcefulness as a stained glass artist, as well as to his unstinting helpfulness, patience, and endurance. And because his knowledge of the Keck Studio from the day he joined it in 1922—and even earlier—is astonishingly complete, it is fair to say that no study of the Studio could have been successful without his full participation. And heartfelt thanks also go to Mrs. Minnie Worden for her ever-gracious patience and hospitality in allowing us to invade her home with notebooks, cameras, recorders, and endless questions for her husband.

Everyone concerned with the history of the Studio owes a great debt of gratitude to Henry Keck's daughters, Myra Keck Betters and Alice Keck Plassche, and his son-in-law, Walter Plassche. They have helped the project enormously in many ways, not least in sharing their memories and lending memorabilia and works of art. Professor Helen Zakin, a scholar of stained glass, has not only contributed a chapter to this book but has also generously provided expert advice to the other researchers on many points. From the very beginning of planning for the Keck Studio exhibition, graphic designer Norman Abrams and photographer Courtney Frisse offered valuable guidance in both conceptual and practical matters. Many of Courtney Frisse's photographs, taken originally for the exhibition, now illustrate this book.

Among the dozens of individuals and groups who provided information, advice, hospitality, moral support, hands-on help, loans of works of art, and product donations to the entire project from its conception, through its research and development, to the completion of the exhibition and this book, a few must be singled out for special thanks. These include Mrs. Hans Brand, the late Marion Kelso, Margaret Shepard, and William Yost, all formerly of the Keck Studio; Stanton Catlin, William Fleming, Laurence Kinney, Sally Kohlstedt, Coy L. Ludwig, Frank Macomber, Mary Ann Smith, and David Tatham; Richard Wright and Violet Hosler of the Onondaga Historical Association; Frances and Anthony Terino; Joyce Ross; Steve Wright, Rebecca Lawton, Sue Williams, and Ralph Swalm III; Elizabeth Gilmore Holt; Allan Sustare and the Studio Gallery; Jules Fox and the Norwich Jewish Center; James G. Gies; the late Burton Blatt; Father Stephen Rossey; Ann Hutchinson; Edward Joy Company, Syracuse Blueprint Company, Glundal Color Corporation, Midstate Printing Corporation, Industrial Color Labs, and Silverman Mower Advertising. Thanks go, too, to the Office of the Chancellor of Syracuse University.

Donald Pulfer, former Programs Director for IDEA, deserves special thanks for his constant support and helpful advice over the years, as do William Fisher and Gail Wiltshire, Directors of IDEA, who aided the completion of this project in many ways beyond the call of duty.

Finally, thanks must go to the many persons—clerics, stained glass makers, and others—who allowed the authors access to buildings, windows, and memories of Henry Keck and his legacy of beauty.

Syracuse, New York   CLEOTA REED
Summer 1984

Introduction

HE HENRY KECK STAINED GLASS STUDIO was one of the more important enterprises contributing to upstate New York's extraordinary part in the Arts and Crafts Movement in America. Though it was established in 1913, after the Arts and Crafts Movement was in full flower, many factors link it to the crafts community which nurtured the ideologies of John Ruskin and William Morris and brought them to a second season of fruition, this time in New York State soil.

Throughout England in the late nineteenth century, many viewers found an indictment of the Industrial Revolution and its unfilled promise of a better life in the degradation of design in manufactured objects. Careless workmanship was brought about by a division of labor which reduced factory work to meaningless and repetitive tasks, deplorable working conditions for factory employees, and an increasingly polluted environment. Ruskin and his disciple, Morris, were among the important intellectuals, artists, and craftsmen calling for reform and a return to the preindustrial values of simplicity, honesty, and integrity. Their ideas spawned the Arts and Crafts Movement.

Ruskin, fifteen years Morris' senior, decried the fact that manual labor and intellectual labor were becoming increasingly separated, and he urged a return to the medieval guild system of production in which the worker-craftsman was involved with the process from design to finish. A greater theoretician than political activist, Ruskin was an advocate for the Gothic style, a style which he said derived its expressiveness from the hands of the hundreds of individual medieval workmen, not precise machines, who cut and laid the stones of the Gothic cathedrals. He held the belief that art reflects the kind of society that produces it, and he felt that the advent of the machine age had brought design in England to a low ebb.

Morris, generally considered the leading light of the Arts and Crafts Movement in England, had no interest in reconciling art and industry. To Morris and his colleagues, "Art . . . meant individuality and the search for 'truth', whether in painting, architecture or applied design—and truth, they felt, could be found both in the study of nature and in the re-creation of the spirit rather than the letter of medievalism. Direct imitation of the Gothic was meaningless."[1] With several partners Morris in 1861 formed the firm of Morris, Marshall, Faulkner and Company (later known simply as Morris and Company). Members of the firm also included the painters Dante Gabriel Rossetti, Edward Burne-Jones, and Ford Madox Brown, as well as the architect Philip Webb. The outstanding products of Morris and Company usually reflected direct, honest workmanship and design based on the study of natural forms. The firm produced simple, workaday furniture as well as elegant and elaborate state furniture. Among their products were wallpaper, chintzes and other fabrics, rugs, tapestries, embroideries, furniture, ceramics, pottery, tiles, and stained glass.

Morris, a dedicated socialist, spent much of his time working for causes which he thought would enable the common man to find greater pleasure in his life and work. His *News from Nowhere* (1890) was an idyllic version of a socialist rural utopia resembling, to a point, the numerous communities and guilds that were associated with the Arts and Crafts Movement in England. In 1890 Morris established the Kelmscott Press, the focus of his creative activity for the remainder of his life. Kelmscott Press books, in which type, spacing, illustrations, ink, and paper were conceived of as an integral unit, created a new aesthetic for printing and publishing.

Beginning as early as 1876, when American design made a generally poor showing at the Centennial Exposition in Philadelphia, there had been a growing awareness of America's shortcomings in the design of manufactured goods. A conscientious effort was begun to improve the situation, especially in the teaching of applied arts and manual training. When the aspiring writer Elbert Hubbard, recently retired from a highly successful sales and executive position with the Larkin Soap Manufacturing Company in Buffalo, decided to make a grand tour of Europe, he was particularly receptive to the Arts and Crafts activities taking place in England, where, in 1894, he met with Morris. Upon his return to his home in East Aurora later that year, Hubbard printed his first booklet, *A Little Journey to the Home of George Eliot*, thus taking the initial step toward establishing what was probably the first consciously planned Arts and Crafts organization in upstate New York, the Roycroft Community.

Unlike the utopian religious communities of the Shakers and the

Oneida Community which earlier had established bases in New York State, the Roycroft Community was loosely patterned along the lines of the medieval guilds, with the central theme being purposeful work, not religion. While the mainstay of the Roycroft Community was its publishing business, including periodical publications such as the *Little Journeys*, *The Philistine*, and *The Fra*, its workshops soon began to produce furniture, metalwork, tooled leather, terra cotta ware, and other goods. Several hundred workers were employed by the Roycroft Shop during its peak years. The enormous success of the organization depended largely upon the charismatic personality of its leader, who was equally effective at selling the Roycroft philosophy as he had been at selling Larkin Soap. In his history of the Roycroft Shop, published in 1908, Hubbard wrote:

> At the Roycroft Shop the workers are getting an education by doing things. Work should be the spontaneous expression of man's best impulses. . . . To develop the brain we have to exercise the body. To develop the mind, we must use the body. Manual training is essentially moral training; and physical work is at its best mental, moral and spiritual.
>
> At the Roycroft Shop we are reaching out for an all-round development through work and right living. And we have found it a good expedient —a wise business policy. Sweat-shop methods can never succeed in producing beautiful things. And so the management of the Roycroft Shop surrounds the workers with beauty, allows many liberties, encourages cheerfulness and tries to promote kind thoughts, simply because it has found that these things are transmuted into goods, and come out again at the finger-tips of workers in beautiful things.[2]

The Roycroft Community continued to exist into the 1930s, although it suffered a severely crippling blow in 1915 when Hubbard died in the sinking of the *Lusitania*. At least two other Arts and Crafts communities were established in New York State in the early years of the twentieth century—Byrdcliffe, near Woodstock, in 1902 and the Elverhöj Colony at Milton-on-Hudson in 1913. The existence of these communities indicates to some degree the Arts and Crafts activity taking place in New York at the turn of the century; however, far more numerous than the communities were the individuals who established studios, workshops, training programs, and publishing concerns there in pursuit of the crafts. Their important influence on the quality of design and production techniques was evidenced for several decades.

One of the major forces was Charles Fergus Binns, who in 1900 became the first director of the New York State School of Clayworking and Ceramics at Alfred. Through his numerous students at both the regular sessions and the Alfred summer school, his vast technical knowledge of ceramics was dispersed to the leading American art pottery studios, including Marblehead, Newcomb, Overbeck, Robineau, and Pewabic. Another towering figure in the Arts and Crafts Movement in New York was Adelaide Alsop Robineau, who, with her husband Samuel Robineau, began publishing the monthly *Keramic Studio* in Syracuse and New York City in 1899. Initially oriented toward the popular handicraft of china painting, *Keramic Studio* quickly became a leading publication for the serious studio potter. Mrs. Robineau's own work in porcelain was unparalleled in America. Frederick Walrath, a former student of Binns, left the Grueby Pottery Company of Boston to head the ceramics department at the Mechanics Institute in Rochester in 1908. He achieved considerable recognition both as a teacher and as a studio potter.

The Mechanics Institute (now Rochester Institute of Technology), established in 1885, represented the area's response to the need and concern for adequate facilities for the training of professional designers and technicians. At a more popular level, the theories postulating the importance of developing both the intellectual and manual capabilities of students were reflected in New York State's passage of a bill in 1888 authorizing the establishment of departments for teaching and illustrating the industrial or manual arts in its public and normal schools. The Manual Training Movement, while not a direct outgrowth of the Arts and Crafts Movement, stemmed from some of the same concerns and shared with it many common aims.

The School of Design and Arts of the Mechanics Institute was housed after 1910 in a building designed by one of Rochester's leading architects of the Arts and Crafts period, Claude Bragdon, also a talented writer and illustrator. His contributions ranged from illustrations for one of the better-known of the little magazines, *The Chap Book*, to the design for the magnificent New York Central Railroad Station in Rochester, now demolished. The architect's masterpiece, the railroad station was based on the geometry of musical ratios and was lavishly decorated with Grueby tiles. Harvey Ellis, a Rochester friend and colleague of Bragdon, was a skillful and sensitive designer who brought a unique sophistication to his many projects, whether architectural renderings and furniture designs or illustrations and watercolors. Ellis is perhaps best known for the work he produced during one short year (1903–1904) at *The Craftsman* magazine in Syracuse and for the influence his exceptional ability had on the magazine and its publisher, Gustav Stickley.

The figure in the American Arts and Crafts Movement whose position most closely approximates that of William Morris in the movement in England was Gustav Stickley. Designer, manufacturer, philosopher, builder, promoter—Stickley was the consummate craftsman. His radically new structural or mission style oak furniture, produced in Eastwood (then a suburb, now part of Syracuse), was introduced at a 1900 trade fair in Grand Rapids.[3] To the "tasteful" eye accustomed to ornateness and excess, the simplicity of this direct, structural style must truly have been shocking. Within a year of introducing this new furniture, Stickley had opened new headquarters in the Craftsman Building in downtown Syracuse and, with ample assistance from Syracuse University professor Irene Sargent, had begun publication of *The Craftsman* magazine which would become the voice of the Arts and Crafts Movement in America. The details of Stickley's career in Syracuse and New York City during the *Craftsman* years, 1901–1916, are generally known, but the scope of his enormous influence continues to reveal itself as research on the Arts and Crafts Movement continues.

In 1903, following the lead of the Arts and Crafts Exhibition Society in England (1888) and the Society of Arts and Crafts, Boston (1897), Stickley organized and presented at the Craftsman Building in Syracuse the first major Arts and Crafts exhibition to be held in upstate New York. The exhibition, remarkable for the variety and quality of objects presented, traveled to the Mechanics Institute in Rochester after its Syracuse showing, where it was reorganized and enlarged by Theodore Hanford Pond. From the Maison Bing in Paris to the Fireside Industries of Berea College in Kentucky, the producers of outstanding Arts and Crafts were represented in categories that included pottery, decorative metalwork, gold and silver work, decorative leather, bookbinding, printing, Indian handicrafts, textiles, furniture, and stained glass. The European work, according to Irene Sargent writing in *The Craftsman*, had been selected by Stickley during a recent visit to England and France.

In the Syracuse exhibition, work from four stained glass studios was shown: Church Glass Company, New York City; Charles J. Connick, Pittsburg; Margaret Redmond, Philadelphia; and J. and R. Lamb, New York City. It is not unreasonable to imagine that a young Henry Keck might have participated in the design and/or production of the "Casement Windows in Opalescent Glass" exhibited by the Lambs for, as Dorothy Terino indicates in her history of the Keck Stained Glass Studio, it was at about this time that

Keck was employed by J. and R. Lamb, the oldest existing American stained glass studio.

When Henry Keck opened his studio in Syracuse in 1913, the Arts and Crafts Movement had been flourishing in upstate New York for more than fifteen years. One assumes that at least part of his reason for settling here was the potential market for stained glass to be used in the windows, cabinets, and doors of Arts and Crafts homes—from bungalows to English cottages. Certainly many of his early commissions came from Ward Wellington Ward, Syracuse's outstanding architect of the period, whose designs often combined honestly presented natural building materials with Moravian tiles and Henry Keck stained glass to create an "Arts and Crafts ideal." [4]

Henry Keck learned about stained glass making in its entirety through an apprenticeship, begun at the age of fourteen, at the Tiffany Studios in New York. This method of instruction, common in the medieval guilds, had begun to die out during the Industrial Revolution but had been revived in England as part of the Arts and Crafts approach to work and manual training. By studying every aspect of stained glass, Keck knew the process from design to production to installation. And Keck operated his own studio in Syracuse not as a factory but as a workshop of craftspersons, a method that would have met with John Ruskin's approval. Producing stained glass was a team effort, and capable artists and artisans, often initially hired as apprentices, learned and participated in many phases of the process.

When Stanley Worden, who eventually was to become chief designer and director, joined the Keck Studio in 1922, he came as an apprentice artist, fresh from the manual training and mechanical drawing classes at the Syracuse Vocational High School—a shining example of manual training's effectiveness. Through skill, study, diligence, and the love of his work, he advanced to the position of greatest responsibility at the Studio and earned the respect and admiration of his colleagues in the stained glass industry.

Although the Keck Studio was established in 1913, well after many of the radical aspects of Arts and Crafts design and thought had come to be accepted as the norm, and continued production into the 1970s, when the movement was beginning to be studied as a historical phenomenon, its work exemplified those qualities of craftsmanship, fitting design, and integrity that are identified with the Arts and Crafts Movement. The early stained glass produced by the Keck Studio—like an exquisitely carved porcelain by Adelaide Robineau, a uniquely stylized rendering by Harvey Ellis, a classic oak chair by Gustav Stickley, or a piece of hammered metalwork from the Roycroft Shop—has come to be regarded as an important manifestation of the

Arts and Crafts Movement in upstate New York. Henry Keck's work continues to enrich our environment and our lives. The chapters which follow contribute significantly to our further understanding and appreciation of this important stained glass artist.

COY L. LUDWIG

NOTES

1. Gillian Naylor, *The Arts and Crafts Movement: A Study of its Sources, Ideals and Influence on Design Theory* (Cambridge, MA: MIT Press, 1971), p. 101.

2. Elbert Hubbard, *The Roycroft Shop, Being a History* (East Aurora: Roycroft, 1908), pp. 26–27.

3. Mary Ann Smith, *Gustav Stickley, The Craftsman* (Syracuse: Syracuse University Press, 1983), p. 23.

4. Cleota Reed Gabriel, *The Arts and Crafts Ideal: The Ward House—An Architect and His Craftsmen* (Syracuse: IDEA, Inc., 1978), p. 14.

HENRY KECK STAINED GLASS STUDIO, 1913–1974

A Brief History

DOROTHY FRANCES TERINO

HE YEAR 1913 was important in the history of art in Syracuse, New York, for it was then that the stained glass artist Henry Keck established his business there.

The Henry Keck Studio was to produce outstanding artwork in stained glass over a period that spanned seven decades. Under Keck's leadership and later under Stanley Worden's, the Studio made windows of such quality that it attracted clients from many parts of the country. In cities and towns in thirty-seven states there are churches, synagogues, public buildings, and private residences that have been enhanced by the colorful stained glass windows created by Keck, Worden, and the artists and artisans who worked with them.

Although American stained glass has been widely admired for the contribution it has made to our environment, art historians have not given this art the study it deserves. Perhaps this is because stained glass making is a business as well as an art. Whatever the reason, the talented individuals and studios that created these works of art have generally remained unknown and unappreciated.

In the case of the Henry Keck Studio, we are extremely fortunate to have an extensive archive of its production. Stanley Worden, who inherited the directorship when Keck died in 1956, had the wisdom to retain the records of the Studio. Because Worden saw the value of this material—record ledgers, correspondence, order books and job accounts (including employee assignments and time schedules), watercolor sketches, full-size cartoons, photographs of the studio and slides of the work, scrapbooks, other business documents, tools and materials (including samples of glass of all types, some of which are no longer made) of the trade, and studio memorabilia—we are able to reconstruct the history of the Keck Studio. Many of the Studio's most important windows are documented at every stage of development from initial letter of inquiry through design to final installation. Such a collection of materials and records is an unusual phenomenon in the stained glass business. Its value to the study of the history of the stained glass industry in America is inestimable.[1]

The Keck Studio produced a remarkable variety of artwork in a period of near constant change and turmoil. The years from 1913 until 1974, when the Studio closed, were marked by two world wars, the Depression, undreamed-of advances in science and technology, and tremendous social upheavals. People's tastes changed in almost every aspect of life, including art and design. The Keck Studio responded so flexibly to changing styles, tastes, and economic conditions that its output represents quite clearly the range of changes in the entire stained glass industry.

The last quarter of the nineteenth century marked America's coming of age in the decorative arts. The transformation from an agricultural into an industrial nation brought extraordinary changes, among them rapid urbanization, enormous increases in population, and unprecedented economic growth. With this metamorphosis there emerged a budding sense of a unique and special "American" culture. At a time when a taste for sumptuous rich ornament and decoration was greater than in any other period, and the decorative arts were flourishing, America began to reject the domination of Europe to look to its own artists and craftsmen.

Two very important figures in this native flowering of the decorative arts were Louis Comfort Tiffany (1848–1933), and John La Farge (1835–1910). Stimulated by the aesthetic possibilities of rich and luminous colored glass, each developed new techniques for manipulating glass to produce novel and interesting effects.

Tiffany's experiments in glass technology and his successes in Art Nouveau design brought him to the forefront in the production of stained and opalescent glass. The Tiffany stained glass studio in Manhattan expanded to enormous size to accommodate the popular demand for its windows and decorative pieces. By the turn of the century many of the glass artists in America had worked for Tiffany in some capacity at one time or another. Waves of immigration brought thousands of skilled workers into New York from Europe, and Tiffany tapped this pool for talented craftsmen.

Henry Keck, Sr., a German who had owned a millwork business in Giessen, was one of the many who left Germany during the economic turmoil of the last quarter of the nineteenth century. In 1880, at the age of forty-three, he came to America with his wife and seven children and soon found work at the Tiffany studio making sash and installing windows.

In 1887, when an apprenticeship position became available at Tiffany's, Henry Keck, Jr., aged fourteen, applied and was hired. [2] Henry Jr.'s apprenticeship exposed him to all aspects of stained glass making at Tiffany's. He learned the mechanical and technical skills of the trade, especially lead glazing. Here, in Keck's own words, he was involved with "some of the most beautiful work that firm has ever turned out. It was wonderful training." [3] His early exposure to the beauty of stained glass inspired in young Keck a desire to devote himself to its creation. He wanted to be more than a stained glass artisan, however; he wanted to be an artist. In his hours off, to develop his skills, he attended evening classes, reportedly at the Art Students' League and the Academy of Design. [4]

During his early years of work, Keck gave all his earnings to his parents, but in his later teens he began to put money aside to further his professional training. In 1895 he returned to Germany to study art in Munich, as well as to gain further experience in his trade. While in Europe he also broadened his knowledge through travel.

Returning to America in 1897, Keck found jobs difficult to come by, since the country was then in an economic slump. He wrote more than one hundred letters of application to stained glass studios throughout the country. For a time he supported himself by painting elaborate Easter eggs. A firm in Chicago finally hired Keck, and he was there long enough to know it was not his style of work. It involved a kind of "factory production" using stock designs. He finally resigned and after traveling from city to city for a while, working on a free-lance basis, he returned to New York City. There he worked first for the J. and R. Lamb Studio, an old established firm, and then later was employed in the art department of the Montague Castle Stained Glass Studio.

In 1903, Keck married Myra Graff, pianist for the Liederkranz singing group to which he belonged. They had four children—a son, born in 1904 who died two years later, and three daughters, Myra, Elisabeth, and Alice.

Sometime between 1909 and 1911 Keck accepted a position with the Pike Stained Glass Studio in Rochester, New York. Keck had been an apprentice glazier with Pike at the Tiffany Glass Company many years before. In Rochester, Pike put him in charge of the studio's art work.

In April of 1913 Keck opened his own stained glass studio in Syracuse. He was now forty years of age. With the money he had saved and with funds he borrowed, probably from his brother Charles, a well-known New York sculptor, he had $40,000 in capital to back up his venture.

Keck apparently selected Syracuse for the site of his new business because of its central location in New York State and because the Pike Studio in Rochester was getting a great deal of work in the area, a clear indication of business opportunity. Keck's choice was a sound one, as Syracuse was a vital and growing city that welcomed new business. In the Central New York region in 1913, stained glass was manufactured in Utica, where there were two or three studios, and in Rochester, where there was Pike. In thriving, progressive Syracuse there was no stained glass studio, and this fact influenced Keck's decision to open a studio there.

In addition to the business advantages that it offered, Syracuse had a medical center, a widely respected university, and a sizeable German population with its own German-language weekly newspaper. All of these features must have impressed Keck favorably.

A further incentive surely was the fact that Syracuse had become a fertile center of the Arts and Crafts Movement in America (*Plate 1*). Gustav Stickley had his furniture-making establishment in nearby Eastwood. His magazine, *The Craftsman*, a nationally recognized forum for the ideals of the movement, was published here. Adelaide Alsop Robineau, an internationally known potter, lived and worked in Syracuse. Ward Wellington Ward, a prolific Central New York Arts and Crafts architect, practiced in the area.[5]

Although Syracuse was an advantageous location, Keck faced a difficult struggle. As late as 1913, the American stained glass business remained in the shadow of its European competition despite the strides of Tiffany and La Farge. Most important commissions still went to European studios.[6] These studios were adept at producing the traditional styles required by the Neo-Gothic church architecture of the period, and a European imprint still conveyed a sense of quality and authenticity for many American clients.

The most important advantage held by the European studios, however, was the cost. They could produce finished windows for less because the wages paid European craftsmen were lower. Moreover, the American studios had to import most of their glass thereby adding to their costs of manufacture. The import tariff on European windows was not high enough to offset these disadvantages to the American studios, and some American craftsmen even set up studios in Europe to make windows for the American market.[7]

In 1913, because of political pressure from importers and church leaders, Congress lowered the tariff by one-third. This bill probably would have ruined the American stained glass industry had it not been for the trade embargo which was imposed at the outbreak of World War I. This embargo temporarily freed the American studios from their European competition.

Keck's business in the early years probably benefitted from the embargo: it very likely brought him commissions which previously would have gone to European studios. Nevertheless, only the fittest could survive the economic problems confronting the American stained glass industry. Keck proved to be one of the fittest. He had the wide experience, training, artistic talent, business acumen, and personality needed for success.

Keck established his studio in Syracuse in April of 1913 in a rented building at 120 West Jefferson Street. Several years later he moved to the third story of B. F. Metcalf & Son, 216 West Genesee Street, and in 1924 he purchased the Powell Nursery property at what is now 1010 West Genesee Street. With the aid of Syracuse architect Howard B. Yates, he had the building remodeled and enlarged to accommodate his shop. This building remained the home of the Henry Keck Studio for half a century.

Keck followed the practice of most twentieth-century stained glass firms in dividing the work along the lines of studio and shop. The artists in the studio designed windows, produced watercolor sketches and drawings, selected glass colors and/or painted glass. The craftsmen in the shop cut glass pieces, fired the kilns, leaded the windows and installed them. The quality of the Studio's work depended, of course, on the skills and teamwork of its members. To do the shopwork, Keck hired Robert Steinmiller and Albert Jensen in 1913. Both had worked with him at the Pike Studio. Soon afterward, he brought in Grover Hyatt, another Rochester colleague, as shop foreman. These three composed the core of Keck's early staff.[8]

Soon after opening his business, Keck contacted all of the architects in the area to acquaint them with his new studio because he realized that more work could be anticipated from an architect than from an individual client. Keck also made himself visible in the community. He joined the Free and Accepted Order of Masons, the Syracuse Museum of Fine Arts, and the Rotary Club. He served as a deacon and elder in the First Presbyterian Church. These memberships yielded a large body of friends and acquaintances. Through his natural gregariousness and his ability to converse easily on any subject, Keck established a personal rapport with people which helped him in winning commissions.

Not much is known about the early years of the Keck Studio, for few records before 1930 have survived. Keck's first entry in the Syracuse City Directory of 1915 listed "Memorial Church Windows in Painted Antique or Opalescent Glass; Ornamental, Domestic Leaded Glass; Mosaics;

Lamp Shades."[9] This supports what Keck's training suggests and what his work reveals: he was producing windows and lampshades in the rich opalescent style of Tiffany. In addition to work in the Tiffany style, Keck produced glass in the more simplified Arts and Crafts idiom, and windows in the medieval painted ecclesiastical style (*Plates 2 and 3*). This versatility is the mark of a good businessman. It was a continuing characteristic of the Keck Studio.

The first entry in Keck's sales and expense ledger was for the repair of a lampshade, paid on June 13, 1913. He was soon repairing windows, replacing panels in Wurlitzer music boxes, and supplying glass to Gustav Stickley, probably for making lamps.[10] He received orders regularly from the lumber companies and hardware stores for leaded diamond-paned windows and house "lights" (windows) within a month after he was in business.

The first major commission Keck won after opening his studio was for a church in Spencer, New York, where he made at least three windows: a *Good Samaritan*, a *Guardian Angel*, and an *Adoration of the Shepherds*, all in opalescent glass. According to Keck's sales and expense ledger, this set of windows was installed in September 1913. Other jobs followed in quick succession, and Keck's reputation began to spread beyond New York State. Notable early jobs were for the Calvary Baptist Church in Syracuse (*Figure 2*), the First Methodist Church in Newark, New Jersey, and St. Mary's Academy in Leavenworth, Kansas.

In 1917 Keck undertook an unusual and prestigious commission in Claymont, near Wilmington, Delaware (*Plate 4*). In ten weeks he designed, fabricated, and installed a moveable stained glass covering, forty-eight feet square. This was created for the interior court of Archmere, the elaborate million-dollar villa of Jacob Raskob, an officer of the DuPont Corporation. Using thousands of pieces of opalescent glass in the skylight, Keck designed a grape arbor with brilliantly colored exotic birds in the foliage. A sunburst radiates from the center to the surrounding arbor.[11]

Besides his regular staff, Keck also used free-lance craftsmen and laborers whenever he needed them. He guaranteed them work for a limited time, often hiring them for specific projects. In the skylight executed for the Raskob villa, Keck had twelve or thirteen workmen assisting him. As business warranted, Keck occasionally hired other artists to design windows. Charles Young, a Syracuse painter, and Norman Lindner, head artist for Pike, were both employed by Keck at times on a free-lance basis (*Figure 3*). For the most part his regular staff in the early years consisted of only himself and his three employees.

The work of the Studio became more widely known as Keck pre-

Figure 2. Christ, The Good Shepherd. Opalescent window for Calvary Baptist Church, Syracuse, New York. Designed and painted by Henry Keck. 1915. Photo, Cleota Reed.

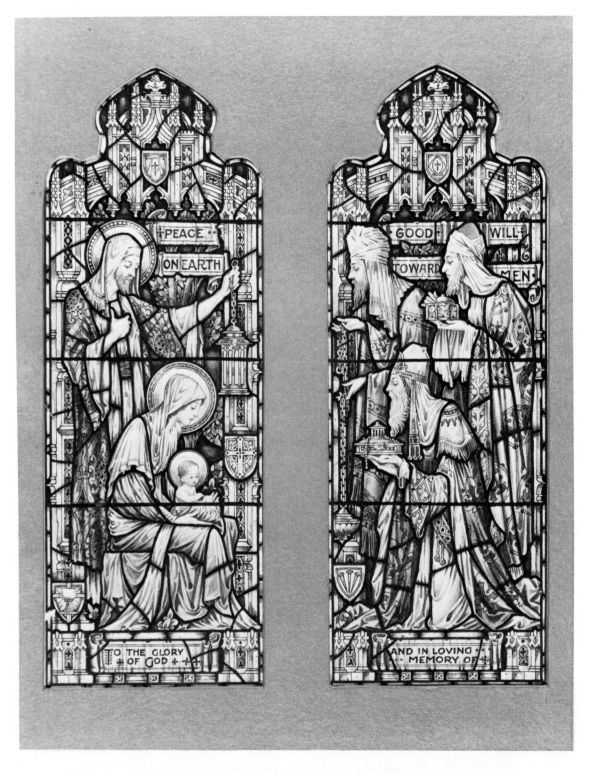

Figure 3.   Adoration of the Magi. Sepia and ink sketch, 8 x 6⅝ inches. Design for two-panel Neo-Gothic window. Norman Lindner. Circa 1930. Private collection. Photo, 1983. Courtney Frisse. An artist with the Pike Studio in Rochester, Lindner did free-lance work for Keck. This drawing was made in sepia and ink to be photographed for a portfolio for the Keck Studio rather than for an actual job. Lindner's exquisite drawings served as important models for the young apprentice Stanley Worden in the early 1920s.

pared windows for local churches. By 1918 Keck's reputation as a superb craftsman was well established. A Syracuse newspaper of that year proclaimed that Keck's "fame" for stained glass was nationwide.[12] In time most of the churches of the Syracuse area were to have windows made by Henry Keck and his staff.

Although the creation of windows for religious buildings had always been the backbone of the stained glass business, a large part of the work, both before and after World War I, was for homes and other secular buildings. Many of the architects of that period, including Frank Lloyd Wright, recommended stained glass for domestic architecture both to provide ornamentation and to eliminate the need for blinds. In 1920 Keck himself observed that "while the churches will doubtless furnish the stained glass artist with his chief commissions for many years, there is a growing appreciation among the American people of the beauties of this glass for home decoration purposes."[13]

The Keck Studio produced many lovely residential windows. Two windows for the Dr. Charles Blum residence in Syracuse are particularly fine examples from the mid-1920s. Designed by Gustav Bernhardt, an artist then in the Keck employ, one three-panel window entitled *Hollyhocks (Plate 5)*, is reminiscent of early Tiffany designs. The second three-panel window depicts a Pre-Raphaelite female, *Maid of the Earth (Plate 6)*. Another outstanding example of the Keck Studio domestic windows is a series of "Rathskeller" windows depicting various pleasures of life *(Plate 7)*. These panels were designed in the 1930s by Stanley Worden for M. C. Eaton in Norwich, New York.

The First World War had been a boon to the American stained glass trade; the embargo had given it a chance to prove itself. America's monopoly at home did not last. As the nations recovered from the unsettling effects of the war, foreign competition returned. The best American studios, however, Keck's among them, had shown that they could match the quality of European work.

The boom in construction after the war brought much work to the Studio. Church commissions increased in number. Lumber companies kept the Studio busy with orders for residential windows of simple geometric patterns or ornamental designs in clear glass. The Studio made as many as a hundred of these a week.

In the twenties, as business increased, Keck enlarged his staff. Although he had said that American craftsmen were equal to those of Europe, Keck did not hesitate to advertise in foreign newspapers when he needed skilled and thoroughly trained artisans. In 1923 Keck hired Hans Brand, a

German glass craftsman who was working in The Hague at the time. The English artist Thomas Porter arrived from New York City in 1924 to serve as head designer (*Plate 8*). For about two years, 1925–1927, the German artist Gustav Bernhardt served on the staff doing excellent ornamental work.

Keck also hired several local boys as apprentices. In 1922 he employed George Greer as apprentice glazier and glass cutter and a seventeen-year-old high school student, Stanley Worden, as artist's apprentice. In 1924 Keck hired another youth, sixteen-year-old William Yost, to learn the mechanical skills of the trade.

Of the many Keck Studio employees hired during its sixty-one years of operation, a small number provided continuity. The head artists were Henry Keck (1913–1924), Thomas Porter (1924–1929), and Stanley Worden (1929–1974). The shop foremen were Grover Hyatt (1913–1929), Hans Brand (1929–1967), and William Yost (1967–1971). These six men comprised the backbone of the Studio during its long history. Brand served the Studio for more than forty years while Yost and Worden remained for about half a century.

Although Keck cannot have realized it for some years, his hiring of Stanley Worden was to have an incalculable impact on the Studio. In time Worden would succeed Keck as director, but even in the 1920s his work as a designer and painter enhanced the artistic strength of the Studio.

When he answered Keck's advertisement for a boy with artistic ability, Worden brought to the interview a portfolio containing the assignments he had completed for a home study art course, an oil painting he had done five years earlier, some mechanical drawings made in class at Syracuse Vocational High School, and some cartoons he had drawn. [14]

Worden began his Studio training with such menial tasks as sweeping the floor and washing pieces of glass. The boy was soon laying out pieces of glass on an easel, waxing them on, and transferring them onto trays for firing. He learned to fire the kiln and to construct the lead lines for simple designs. He was taught to design and letter inscriptions by Keck's niece, Hilde Lindenthal, an art school graduate.

Recognizing Worden's innate ability, Keck took a fatherly interest in the young man and urged him to draw at home after work. He pressed Worden to copy, rather than trace, illustrations from books and magazines, and he paid him one dollar for each completed copy. Although the young man had to spend fifteen to twenty hours on each illustration, the experience not only helped to develop Worden's ability to draw and design, but also increased his knowledge of iconography and style and deepened his understanding of stained glass art. [15]

Keck soon taught Worden to do stencil work, sketch cartoons for simple ornamental designs, and later to paint glass. When Thomas Porter joined the Studio, Keck urged Worden to study his painting technique and to learn all he could from him. The older opalescent style, of which Keck was a master, was now falling from fashion, and the newer taste for the revival of Neo-Gothic painted antique glass required skills that Keck could not teach as easily as Porter.

Worden's work improved dramatically. By 1926 he was proficient in watercolor design. The watercolor "sketch" is essentially a detailed design in scale for a stained glass window (*Plate 9*). The lead lines are indicated. The completed watercolor is often varnished to simulate glass and matted to suggest the architectural context. Keck used these watercolor sketches to sell ideas for windows to prospective clients. The more they could convey the spirit of the proposed window, the better the chance of getting the commission. Since the original design was conceived at this stage, the artist labored over these watercolor renditions for days or even weeks.

In 1926 the Studio was invited to submit designs for stained glass windows for the chapel of Loretto Rest in Syracuse. Keck, Porter, and Worden each prepared watercolor sketches. Worden's design was selected. In recognition of Worden's accomplishment, Keck increased his salary from five to fifteen dollars a week.

With Keck's encouragement, Worden enrolled in evening art courses at Syracuse University in 1926. He pursued these evening studies intermittently until 1932. Through his experience in life drawing classes, he developed the ability to portray the human figure in natural poses. [16]

The stock market crash of 1929 and the subsequent Depression brought to an abrupt halt the abundant business that the Studio had enjoyed since World War I. In that year Porter, the head designer, and Hyatt, the shop foreman, jointly bid on a job, not for the Keck Studio, but for themselves. Keck had also submitted a bid, but because their bid was lower, the two collaborators were awarded the work, and they left Keck's employ to start their own studio. [17]

Finding himself in a difficult plight, Keck promoted Hans Brand to shop foreman and, at the same time, invited Joseph Burion, an old colleague from New York City, to come to Syracuse to serve as head artist. Burion's style proved outdated, and his tenure at the Keck Studio lasted only two years. With commission orders to be filled, Keck then turned to Stanley Worden, now twenty-four years old, and promoted him to the (unofficial) post of head designer, seven years after he had hired him as an apprentice. From this time Keck concerned himself mainly with the business aspects of the Studio.

In 1929 approximately nine hundred stained glass studios operated in the United States. Within the next thirty years, "because of depression, war, and destructive European competition, this number would be reduced by almost 75 percent. Only the hardiest of the old line companies could survive the events of the next several decades."[18] As times became difficult, stained glass art became expendable. The Henry Keck Studio proved, however, to be one of those hardiest stained glass companies which endured.

Keck's enterprise and imagination enabled the Studio to survive the Depression. The city directory of 1929 listed for the first time "mural painting" as one of the services that the Studio provided.[19] As mentioned before, Keck had been giving free-lance work periodically to a local painter named Charles Young. Probably it was this association, along with the diminishing number of stained glass commissions, which prompted him to expand the Studio's scope of work. Few murals were actually painted, however.[20]

In the early 1930s Keck listed his firm in the city directory under "Glass Dealers" rather than "Stained Glass," and for the next few years he did a substantial business selling and installing Vitrolite. This decorative structural glass, used as facing for buildings, became more significant than murals to the survival of the business.[21] The Keck Studio continued to market this material all through the Depression. The Studio's first Vitrolite job was the facing of the Art Deco Niagara Hudson (now Niagara Mohawk) Building on Erie Boulevard in Syracuse. As this glass became more popular as a decorative material, Worden even found himself designing bathrooms. During the same period, the Keck Studio also went into the waterproofing business representing Tremco Caulking Company of Cleveland, Ohio. Dwight Simmons, who had been brought in as a salesman about 1928 (and later married Keck's daughter Elisabeth), was placed in charge of the Tremco and Vitrolite work. The staff glaziers served as caulkers and installers. Simmons brought in enough business to enable the Studio to survive the Depression.

All through the 1930s, Keck continued as a dealer in Vitrolite and Tremco caulking; however, as the country pulled out of the Depression, he gained more commissions for stained glass artwork. By 1939 the Studio's advertisement stressed "memorial church windows in English antique glass," a good indication of the type of work which the market was bearing as well as of the changes in taste which had occurred since the teens.[22]

In the late 1930s, in addition to numerous jobs in New York State, Keck obtained large commissions in Indiana, Ohio, North Carolina, and Maryland. For one of these projects—the First Presbyterian Church in Bowling Green, Ohio—the Keck Studio won in competition against at least twenty other prominent stained glass studios.

Commissions continued to come in during the early 1940s. American stained glass studios which had survived the Depression were now doing quite well. European competition disappeared because the war overseas reduced imports almost to nothing. One of Keck's jobs of this period, St. John's Church in Indianapolis, Indiana, was so large that three kilns were fired simultaneously to keep up with the work.[23] But commissions like this were few, and the work fell off drastically after the United States entered World War II. Not essential to the war effort, stained glass was produced only in limited quantities. Lead and solder became difficult to acquire.[24]

With the end of the war, the work of the Studio picked up rapidly. Henry Keck, now in his early seventies, finally enjoyed real business success. Throughout the country new work, restorations, and repairs had accumulated during the conflict. Furthermore, the economic prosperity that followed the war led to a building boom that included churches. Memorial windows for those who lost their lives in the war were much in demand. One of Worden's prized jobs, the war memorial window for the Church of the Ascension in Rochester, New York, was ordered at this time (1944). Based on standard Christian iconography, it depicts the Archangel Michael destroying Satan in the guise of a serpent (*Plate 10*). Another commission soon after the war, the *Liberty* window for St. Mary's Church in Amsterdam, New York, represents a very different kind of memorial window (*Plate 11*). Images, scenes, and symbols relating to liberty and peaceful coexistence from biblical times to the present are depicted.[25]

In 1949–1950 the Keck Studio was selected to execute windows for the New York State Capitol in Albany. The drawings were made by an Albany artist, David Lithgow (1868–1958).[26] Two semicircular windows of the emblem of New York State were made for the Assembly lobby. Beneath one semicircular window is a two-panel window in which appear, amid an ornamental design, oval portraits of Peter Minuit and DeWitt Clinton, two famous figures in New York State history (*Plate 12*). These windows are somewhat unusual for their period in their combination of antique and opalescent glass.

In 1954 the eighty-one-year-old Keck had the Studio incorporated. In July of the following year his wife, who had been ill for many years, passed away. Keck devoted more time to his work, often staying late and working Saturdays. He was at work, in fact, when he suffered a fatal heart attack. He died on April 11, 1956. *Stained Glass*, the periodical of the Stained Glass Association of America, printed a commemorative obituary on Keck and his work.[27]

Keck's artistic skills had been fundamental to his success. He had an outstanding ability to draw ornament; the notebooks from his student so-journ in Europe show his interest and skills as an ornamentalist. In geometric design of clear leaded glass he was exceptionally gifted.

Keck established high standards of design, craftsmanship, and business conduct for the Studio, and he instilled these standards in his staff. He himself was completely dedicated to hard work and artistic endeavor. Although he was patient with his employees and taught them to do the best they could, he never tolerated poor or sloppy craftsmanship. Whenever a completed work did not meet his high standards, Keck ordered that it be done over, regardless of the time or money it cost. Whether the piece was a small door light for a homey vestibule or an enormous altar window for a cathedral, the work of his studio, as the Studio brochures stated, was made according to the best practices and traditions of the craft.

Keck represented old-fashioned paternalism at its best. He required his employees to buy their own tools, believing that they would then take better care of them. One important tool of the trade, he always told his men, is the broom, and he expected everyone to clean up after himself. In many ways the shop was like a family with Keck as the patriarch—stern, fair, demanding, and yet loving.

Henry Keck founded his Studio and guided it for forty-three years. By making sure that Stanley Worden, his protégé, learned all aspects of the profession, Keck prepared the way for the continued life of his establishment. By 1956 Worden had been the Studio's head designer for a quarter of a century. He had gradually assumed more and more of the managerial responsibilities during Keck's last years. After Keck's death Worden remained chief designer but also became director of the Studio and joined Keck's family as a member of the corporation.

Two months after assuming the directorship, Worden hired as office secretary Margaret Shepard, a dynamic, creative employee, whose service to the Studio proved to be indispensable. She not only ran the office with great efficiency but also helped out in the shop on occasion.

Although the Studio remained busy throughout the 1950s, 1960s and right up to its closing in 1974, conditions were changing. The cost of materials increased, construction of new churches decreased, and large contracts became fewer. Although some new churches provided for stained glass windows in their contracts, these often were the first items eliminated when costs rose higher than expected. The Modern Movement in architecture eschewed ornament, and changing religious attitudes de-emphasized traditional decoration. Most newly constructed church buildings no longer called for windows with pictorial representations of saints or scriptural scenes. The windows that were chosen contained stylized emblems, abstract patterns, or simple rectangular panels of colored glass. When figures were used, the style often was abstract with little of the intricate glass painting of earlier decades. There were exceptions, of course, one notable one being the Church of the Transfiguration in Syracuse (*Plate 13*). Here Worden portrayed the life of Christ in a series of nave windows. Though he treated the backgrounds in a more modern style, his painted figures remain naturalistic. This was a compromise between traditional and modern tastes.

Restoration became a very important part of the Studio's work. The most extensive restoration project undertaken by the Keck Studio was the releading and repairing of all the windows of the great chapel at Duke University in North Carolina (the windows were designed by the Bonawit Studio of New York). This was a twenty-year job, performed every summer from 1952 to 1972. Another major restoration was for the windows of Crouse College at Syracuse University, originally installed in the 1890s. The undertaking was completed between 1963 and 1972. For this job the Studio removed all the windows, replaced broken panes with glass Keck had purchased early in the century, and releaded all the glass. The windows were then waterproofed and reinstalled.

As orders for new church windows declined, the Studio sought to attract more business from other sources. In the early 1970s it promoted small window panels in stained glass for Christmas gifts, but without much success.[28]

Major staff changes occurred frequently between 1950 and 1971. Three of the most experienced senior employees, Steinmiller, Brand, and Yost, retired during this period. Another important change was the hiring of two designers, Ronald Shaw and Ernest Ashcroft. These artists made significant contributions to the Studio during its late period and also relieved Worden of many design responsibilities. Both worked in a more modern style (*Figure 4*). Shaw's designs were bold and linear with a strong Art Deco flavor. Ashcroft's highly decorative and original style was more naturalistic. One of his finest designs is the three-panel *Good Shepherd* made to harmonize with a Tiffany window of an earlier vintage in St. Eustace Episcopal Church in Lake Placid, New York.

By the late 1960s staff changes were so frequent that they began to have a crucial effect on the existence of the Studio. It became very difficult for the firm to attract apprentices. As each experienced staff member resigned or retired, the situation became increasingly critical, for it became impossible to find competent replacements. What had been a staff of eight in 1963 dwindled to three by 1971—Worden, Mrs. Shepard, and, in the

Figure 4. *Adoration of the Magi.* Antique glass window, 24 x 28 inches, for Novitiate Mother House, Third Franciscan Order of St. Anthony, Syracuse, New York. Designed and painted by Ronald Shaw. 1960. Photo, Keck Archives. Ronald Shaw was the only Keck Studio artist whose style was distinctly "modern," having a strong affinity with the *art moderne* style of the 1930s and 1940s. Shaw's work satisfied the Studio's need for modern design.

shop, Harry McClean. Worden made heroic efforts to keep the Studio in operation and managed to carry on for another three years. In 1974 he closed the doors to the Keck Studio forever.[29]

Unlike Henry Keck, who had been trained in the Tiffany studio, in Munich, and in various American studios, Stanley Worden acquired all of his training in the Keck Studio in Syracuse. It was his first and only employer. Worden served in his master's studio for fifty-two years, nine years longer than the master himself. His peers in the stained glass industry in 1974 elected him to honorary life membership in the Stained Glass Association of America, one of only four artists to have been so honored.

During its sixty-one years of existence, the Keck Studio consistently produced stained glass windows of exceptionally high quality. This high quality was the result of a number of factors, among which were carefully thought-out design, masterfully executed glass painting, and aesthetically sensitive selection of glass colors. The Studio showed great versatility in suiting a design to a client. Keck's close supervision, and later that of Worden, assured consistent quality in each finished piece. Pride in work and integrity in all aspects of the business also figured in the Studio's success. Although the Henry Keck Studio is now gone, its work remains available for our appreciation: it left as an enduring testament thousands of beautiful works in stained glass.

MAJOR EMPLOYEES OF THE KECK STUDIO

"Hundreds of men and a few women passed through our doors to work for the Studio but some only stayed a few hours," Stanley Worden stated. Most of the artists and craftsmen who stayed longer and made significant contributions to the Studio's work are included in this list with dates of employment. The following biographical information has been compiled from several sources, including interviews with Worden, other living employees, Keck's daughters, and Mrs. Hans Brand, and correspondence with the late Dwight Simmons.

ERNEST ASHCROFT, *artist,* 1963–1968

Ashcroft was brought to Keck Studio from Belfast, Northern Ireland, where he had been an apprentice of Ronald Shaw. He worked as a designer for about five years, then moved to Winnipeg, Canada, where he helped establish another stained glass studio.

GUSTAV BERNHARDT, *artist,* 1925–1927

An artist from Germany, Bernhardt was hired to do design work, and he proved to be an excellent ornamentalist. He did no glass painting. Bernhardt left to work for the Rambusch Studio in New York City. It was through Bernhardt, who had had his own shop in Germany, that Keck acquired two of the three kilns used by the Studio until it closed *(see Figure 19).*

QUENTIN BLAY, *artist,* late 1950s–1961

An Englishman and glass painter, Blay left to work for another studio and is now with the Henry Willet Studio in Philadelphia.

HANS BRAND, *artist/craftsman,* 1923–1967

Born and educated in Germany, Brand served as a stained glass apprentice there before World War I. After the war he worked in The Hague where he saw one of Keck's advertisements. He began work for the Studio as an "outside" man, installing windows, and later became a glass cutter. When Grover Hyatt left in 1929, Brand was promoted to shop foreman, a position he retained until he retired. He instituted a ledger (now part of the Keck Studio Archive) which documented each job of significance. Having been trained as an artist, Brand shared the responsibility with Worden for selecting glass. After his retirement, he helped occasionally in the Studio. Brand died in 1971.

JOSEPH BURION, *artist*, 1929–1931

Keck hired his old friend from his New York City days to replace Thomas Porter as head artist. Burion's style proved too picturesque and sentimental for the period.

GEORGE GREER, *craftsman*, 1922–c. 1928

Hired as an apprentice glazier and glass cutter, Greer advanced to the rank of journeyman. He left to work with the Collins Paint Shop in Syracuse.

ROBERT (CHUCK) HEIM, *apprentice artist*, 1946–1958

Heim was one of two government-sponsored Navy veterans the Keck Studio hired after World War II. Heim was being trained to eventually replace Worden but left after twelve years to work in New York City.

JACK HILL, *craftsman*, 1957–1965

English trained, Hill answered Keck's advertisement in a Canadian newspaper. He worked as a glass cutter and glazier and left the Studio to become an estimator for the Syracuse Glass Company.

GROVER HYATT, *craftsman*, 1913–1929

One of the first employees of the Studio, Hyatt became shop foreman. He left with Thomas Porter to establish a studio in Connecticut.

ALBERT JENSEN, *craftsman*, 1913–late 1920s.

According to Worden, Jensen, a Dane, was "the world's best" glazier. He came with Keck from the Pike Studio and eventually left to work in New York City.

MARION KELSO (DANN), *artist*, 1932–1950.

A 1932 graduate of the Syracuse University School of Art, Kelso worked sporadically for the Studio for a number of years. For a time she was Worden's apprentice. She was very skilled in lettering and inscriptions. When Daniel Shaw opened his own studio, she was his artist. Kelso died in 1982.

NORMAN LINDNER, *artist*, 1913–1920s.

Lindner had worked with Keck in the Pike Studio in Rochester. Although he remained with Pike as head artist, he often did free-lance work for Keck, perhaps as early as 1913, making a number of cartoons and watercolor sketches.

HAROLD (HARRY) McLEAN, *craftsman*, 1963–1974.

McClean came from Belfast, Northern Ireland, to work for Keck. He was an all-round craftsman, doing glass selection and cutting, glazing, and waterproofing. He was one of the three remaining employees of the Keck Studio when it closed.

THOMAS PORTER, *artist*, 1924–1929.

An Englishman, Porter came from New York City to serve as Keck's head artist. He was considered a fine artist and glass painter. He left to establish a studio in Connecticut, in partnership with Grover Hyatt.

GEORGE RIEGER, *artist,* 1938–1941

Rieger worked primarily painting glass. When Keck discovered that he had Nazi sympathies he fired him.

ADOLPH ROTENECKER, *artist,* 1940s–early 1950s

Rotenecker came from New York City four or five times to work as a free-lance glass painter when the Studio was very busy.

DANIEL (DANNY) SHAW, *craftsman apprentice,* 1946–1955

A Navy veteran, Shaw began his apprenticeship in the shop under a government-sponsored training program. Although Keck intended that Shaw should someday become shop foreman, he left after nine years to establish his own studio and eventually went to work for the Willet Studio in Philadelphia.

RONALD (RONNIE) SHAW, *artist,* 1955–1962

From Belfast, Northern Ireland, Shaw brought thirty years of experience as a stained glass artist. Soon after he arrived, Keck died. Worden became director and had to devote more time to selling windows and running the business, and Shaw took over most of the design responsibilities. Shaw left the Studio when he became ill. He returned to his homeland, where he died.

MARGARET (PEG) SHEPARD, *office manager,* 1956–1974

Peg Shepard began working for the Studio two months after Keck's death. She proved to be remarkably competent, dynamic, and loyal. In addition to running the office where she modernized office procedures, she helped out with various jobs in the art department and the shop. She remained with the Keck Studio for eighteen years until it closed.

DWIGHT SIMMONS, *salesman,* c. 1928–1942

Simmons traveled widely and did much to keep the studio in business during the lean years of the Depression. During that time he also was the Studio's agent for Vitrolite and Tremco Caulking. In 1933 he married Keck's daughter, Elisabeth, who died five years later. Simmons left to become a salesman for American Hospital Supply.

ROBERT STEINMILLER, *craftsman,* 1913–circa 1920, circa 1926–1953

One of the Studio's original employees, Steinmiller too came from the Pike Studio. He worked as a glass cutter and glazier and installed windows. After a short hiatus in California, he returned and remained with the Studio until his retirement.

WILLIAM YOST, *craftsman,* 1924–1971

Hired as a boy apprentice and trained by Grover Hyatt and Hans Brand, Yost was one of the Studio's chief installers of windows for thirty-five years. He became shop foreman when Brand retired and remained such until his own retirement. In retirement, Yost teaches the stained glass craft to senior citizens.

CHARLES YOUNG, *artist,* circa 1913–1933

Young was a mural painter in Syracuse who was occasionally hired by Keck as a free-lance artist to make designs, watercolor sketches, and cartoons.

THE WORK OF THE KECK STUDIO

The design of a stained glass window requires a great deal of thought and artistry. Beyond the abstract spiritual qualities that changing, colored, softened, and filtered light can impart, there are usually specific iconographical requirements which must be satisfied.

Before a window was started, the architect or building committee sometimes gave the Keck Studio a detailed program of themes as well as other guidelines. Commissions for memorial windows would often come with some idiosyncratic desire of the donor, as well as with the usual, rather complex, ecclesiastical and programmatic requirements or restrictions. At other times the Studio itself would be asked to establish an appropriate subject or program.

Since a majority of commissions were for houses of worship, the Studio artists had to be well acquainted with the Bible. Keck was a lifelong student of the Bible. Worden's familiarity with it began as a small boy when his mother read stories and parables from the Bible to him. Nevertheless, some commissions for unusual or unfamiliar subjects required special research. In 1953, for example, Worden spent three days in the library of the Jewish Theological Seminary in New York City to work out the subjects for a series of windows based on the history of the Jewish people. These were installed in the social hall of the Temple Emanu-El in Providence, Rhode Island *(Figure 5)*. Worden again had to do extensive iconographical research for the Trinity Episcopal Church in Syracuse, with its complex symbols surrounding Old Testament and New Testament figures.

Graphic source material was usually closer at hand than the above mentioned examples suggest. A small collection of books and prints was maintained by most stained glass studios. The Keck Studio artists were thoroughly familiar with the history of western art, and reproductions of paintings often provided design sources. Like most studios, the Keck Studio sometimes copied paintings closely, especially in the early years, but more often the sources were freely adapted. Two windows designed by Gustav Bernhardt in the mid-1920s for St. Mary's Church in Gloversville, New York, are based on paintings by Raphael. Fra Angelico-inspired angels appear in windows in several locations. Many studios of the period, to one degree or another, based their *Christ in Gethsemane* windows on a familiar painting by Heinrich Hoffmann. There is a literal version of Holman Hunt's *Light of the World* in Crescent Hill Baptist Church in Louisville, Kentucky, and an interpretation of the work in the Methodist Church in Bridgeport, New York. Both were executed in the late 1950s.

Figure 5. *Jewish Immigrants Arrive in New York* (right). *Theodor Herzl and The Seal of the State of Israel* (left). Watercolor sketch, 5 x 2½ inches. Design for one of a series of fourteen figure panels for the social hall of Temple Emanu-El, Providence, Rhode Island. Stanley Worden. 1953. Keck Archives. Photo, 1983. Courtney Frisse.

Plate 1.   *Landscape.* Irene M. Johnson memorial window. Painted and plated five-lancet opalescent window, 5 x 9 feet, for former chapel of Hospital of the Good Shepherd, now Office of the Dean, School of Education, Huntington Hall, Syracuse University. Designed and painted by Henry Keck. 1917. Photo, 1983. Courtney Frisse.

Plate 2. *St. Cecilia.* Painted, plated opalescent window, 4 feet in diameter, for St. Mary's Roman Catholic Church, Mexico, New York. Designed and painted by Henry Keck. Before 1915. Photo, 1982. Courtney Frisse.

Plate 3.   Christ in the Garden of Gethsemane. Watercolor sketch, 5½ x 13 inches. Design for opalescent window after painting by Heinrich Hoffman. Henry Keck. Before 1920. Keck Archives. Photo, 1983. Courtney Frisse. The figure in the window is after Hoffman, but the background is an original composition. This was a popular subject, requested by many churches. The sketch, which imitates the style of an oil painting, was presented without lead lines. In the actual window layers of opalescent glass (plating) softened the lead lines.

Plate 4.   *Grape Arbor.* Detail of opalescent glass skylight, 48 feet square, for Archmere, then the residence of John Jacob Raskob, now Archmere Academy, Claymont, Delaware. Designed and painted by Henry Keck. 1917. Photo, 1982. Cleota Reed.

Plate 5. *Hollyhocks.* Painted antique glass window, about 7 x 9 feet, for private residence in Syracuse. Designed by Gustav Bernhardt; painted by Thomas Porter and etched by Stanley Worden. 1926. Private collection. Photo, 1982. Courtney Frisse. This subject was popularized by Tiffany early in the century.

Plate 6. *Maid of the Earth.* Painted antique glass window, 9 x 9 feet, for private residence in Syracuse, New York. Designed and painted by Gustav Bernhardt, after *Flora,* a tapestry designed by William Morris and Edward Burne-Jones in 1885. 1926. Private collection. Photo, 1982. Courtney Frisse.

Plate 7.   *Dance.* One of a series of eight antique glass windows, 17 x 15 inches each, for the residence of M. C. Eaton, Norwich, New York, now Norwich Jewish Center. Designed and painted by Stanley Worden. 1933. Collection: Norwich Jewish Center. Photo, 1982. Courtney Frisse.

Plate 8.   Annunciation. One of a series of painted double lancet antique glass windows for Our Lady of Mount Carmel Roman Catholic Church, Gloversville, New York. Designed and painted by Thomas Porter. Circa 1927. Photo, 1982. Courtney Frisse. This pictorial style in figure work is typical of the late 1920s.

Many of the designs were original, of course, though sometimes circumscribed by their subjects: saints and their attributes, for example, lend themselves to only limited interpretation. Still, a really novel approach was sometimes required. Keck designed one window in Sidney, New York, to mark the founding of the First Methodist Church in that community; his window shows Christ talking with a man and woman in colonial garb. Versatility in design was also necessary. Depending on the architectural context and the nature of the commission, the figures could be abstract, thoroughly modern, Gothic, or realistically representational.

Because Worden sometimes drew from life, a Madonna could closely resemble a friend, or a rose from his garden might find its way to a permanent home in a church. In the window he created for the Smith Chapel of the Morristown, New Jersey, Memorial Hospital, Worden included portraits of a staff doctor and nurse.

Though the bulk of the work of the Keck Studio was ecclesiastical, its commissions included windows for public buildings, nursing homes, schools, military bases, hospitals, libraries, residences, and even restaurants. Styles of artwork ranged from Byzantine to Baroque to modern abstraction. Each window was the result of a complex series of requirements, decisions, and responses. The architectural setting, orientation to light, donor, theme, cost, style, design, color, and the personal style of the artist—all were important elements in the window's creation.

Considering the fact that each window of stained glass was designed and executed for a specific setting, it is unfortunate when such a work is removed from its original context and is installed or exhibited elsewhere, stripped of the associations that informed its creation. Such removal is occurring with alarming frequency today. Even worse, however, is the total loss of the windows through the demolition of buildings, vandalism, the effects of weather, improper care, or lack of maintenance.

Stained glass is an important part of our cultural heritage, a record of changing tastes and values, an integral part of some of our most significant architecture. In our rapidly changing visual environment, windows of stained glass should be preserved as enduring elements of color and beauty, preferably in the locations for which they were created. At a time when derelict buildings are increasing in number, it is hoped that the Keck Archive, along with this modest attempt to inform the public about the work of the Keck Studio, will contribute to greater public appreciation, which is a first step toward preservation.

NOTES

1. In 1974, when he closed the studio, Stanley Worden removed the Archives from the Keck Studio to his home, where he kept the cartoons in their original order, arranged by rack number, and made complete lists of their holdings. The Henry Keck Stained Glass Studio Memorial Archive is now located at the Onondaga Historical Association in Syracuse, New York. Through the generous and untiring efforts of Worden, who supervised the move, the original order of the collection has been maintained. Worden also has been an active consultant in an ongoing project to organize, label, and catalogue the collection.

2. Keck, Sr., first encouraged his son Charles (then twelve) to apply. Charles urged his brother Henry to go in his stead. Both of Keck's brothers were to become artists. Charles (1875–1951) was an apprentice to Augustus St. Gaudens and later became an important sculptor. Maxfield (1880–1943) was a successful sculptor of architectural ornament.

3. "Stained Glass Design is Size of City Lot," Syracuse *Herald,* 12 May 1918, Magazine section, p. 4.

4. According to family tradition, Keck studied at the Cooper Union and the Art Students' League. The latter institution reports no official record of Keck as a student but that does not preclude his attendance there. Two newspaper articles from the 1920s and another from 1954 state that Keck studied at both the Art Students' League and the National Academy of Design. As for his studies in Munich, family tradition has it that he studied at the Royal Academy School of Industrial Design; Peg Weiss suggests that this could have been the *Königliche Kunstgewerbe-Schule München,* better translated as the Royal Arts and Crafts (or Industrial Arts) School of Munich.

5. For two of these figures, see Peg Weiss, *Adelaide Alsop Robineau: Glory in Porcelain* (Syracuse: Syracuse University Press, 1981) and Mary Ann Smith, *Gustav Stickley, The Craftsman* (Syracuse: Syracuse University Press, 1983). Also see Cleota Reed Gabriel, *The Arts and Crafts Ideal: The Ward House—An Architect and His Craftsmen,* exhibition catalogue (Syracuse: IDEA, Inc., 1978), for Ward, Keck, and the ceramist Henry Chapman Mercer.

6. This information and much of what follows concerning the history of the Studio come from many interviews with Stanley Worden and Keck's daughters and son-in-law, Myra Betters and Alice and Walter Plassche. The Keck Studio Archive contains more than one hundred hours of interviews taped with Worden from 1978 to 1982.

7. John Gilbert Lloyd, *Stained Glass in America* (Jenkintown, Pa.: Foundation Books, 1963), p. 104. Ludwig von Gerichten, a well-known stained glass artist of the period, was one of those who opened a studio in Europe to benefit from the financial advantage of the location.

8. A list of major Studio employees appears at the end of this chapter.

9. *Syracuse 1913 Directory* (Syracuse: Sampson & Murdock, 1913), p. 1222. Keck placed this display advertisement in addition to listing his form in the city business directory under "Glass Dealers" and "Stained and Cut Glass" until 1931. In 1932 he discontinued the display ad and also the "Stained and Cut Glass" listing, probably to cut his expenses. He continued to list his firm under "Glass Dealers." He resumed listing the studio regularly under "Stained Glass Windows" (and "Glass Dealers") in 1945 but did not place another display ad.

10. Sales and Expense Record, 1913–1923. Keck Archive. This account has helped documentation of some early work. Mary Ann Smith, a scholar of Gustav Stickley, thinks the glass was probably used for lamps, though it could also have been used for panes in prefabricated doors. Both were manufactured by Stickley in the Craftsman Workshop at the time.

11. "Making Stained Glass Covering for New $1,000,000 Villa," Syracuse *Post Standard,* 30 March 1917, p. 14. The Raskob villa is now the home of Archmere Academy. The skylight was restored in the late 1970s by the Henry Willet Studio of Philadelphia.

12. Ibid.

13. "Americans to Hold Stained Glass Trade," Syracuse *Post Standard,* 15 March 1920.

14. Worden's account is worth relating. His Aunt Grace Curtiss and a family friend George Palmer, who was a professional photographer and neighbor and the son-in-law of the Syracuse painter George Knapp, discovered the ad simultaneously and both approached Worden to apply for the position. Like most boys his age, Worden was more interested in playing basketball than in working. Palmer always had taken an interest in Worden and had previously financed his home instruction art course at a cost of five dollars. Worden repaid his debt by carrying out Palmer's ashes at ten cents a haul for fifty weeks. "And there were at least ten heavy loads for each haul," Worden recalled.

15. *International Studio,* a magazine of the decorative arts, was one of these sources. These drawings took him fifteen to twenty hours each to make.

16. His teachers were Syracuse University art professors J. George Hess, Call Tracy Hawley, and Charles Bertram Walker, all of whom placed a great emphasis on academic figure drawing.

17. Porter and Hyatt bid on a job in Cleveland, New York, not for the Keck Studio but for themselves. Keck himself had submitted a bid, but because theirs was low, the two collaborators won the contract. They left Keck to start their own studio, and Keck was furious to lose his head designer and shop foreman in such an underhanded way.

18. Lloyd, *Stained Glass in America,* pp. 106–107.

19. *The Syracuse Directory including Solvay 1929* (Syracuse: Sampson & Murdock, 1929), p. 200.

20. One of these can be seen in Utica, New York, in St. John's Roman Catholic Church.

21. For information about Vitrolite, see *Bulletin: The Association for Preservation Technology 13* (1981).

22. At the turn of the century, many existing stained glass windows were torn out to be replaced by opalescents; then, a generation later, these were in turn replaced in many buildings. Worden recalled being sent in the late 1920s to an upstate church to remove Tiffany windows which were to be replaced by Connick's Neo-Gothic designs. Sometimes the old windows were thrown away.

23. Worden estimated that this Indiana commission required 2,000–3,000 square feet of glass. Worden painted fourteen trays of glass per day.

24. While tin was at a premium throughout the country, Keck was able to obtain old tin pipes from a local junk dealer. Mixing 60 percent tin and 40 percent lead, Keck made his own solder.

25. See Chapter 4 by Cleota Reed in this volume for an analysis of this window.

26. David Lithgow was a friend of Charles Keck. It was through this association that the Studio secured the contract. Charles Keck had also been instrumental in Henry Keck's acquiring the Raskob skylight commission.

27. *Stained Glass* 51 (Spring 1956): 16–17.

28. Advertisement, Syracuse *Herald American*, 10 December 1972.

29. The fate of the Keck Studio has befallen many studios throughout America, except where the skills have been passed on from parent to offspring, as in the case of the Willet Studio in Philadelphia.

2

How the Studio Made Stained Glass

CLEOTA REED

HE KECK STUDIO was in many ways typical of all stained glass studios of its era. The photographs in this chapter, taken there between 1928 and 1966, show activities and settings that were duplicated in dozens of other studios. We see artists and craftsmen plying their skills in an art that has remained virtually unchanged since it originated in the Middle Ages, spacious rooms fitted with broad work tables beside large windows, and works in progress spread on the tables and hung on the windows *(Figure 6)*. What we do not see as readily is the individuality of the Keck Studio and its products, created by artists and craftsmen who worked in age-old traditions to make stained glass windows that were unique, fresh, and of their time.

A stained glass window is a pictorial or ornamental design constructed of hundreds, and sometimes thousands of pieces of colored glass. The colors, ranging from white through most hues of the spectrum, are intrinsic, created by adding metallic oxides to the molten glass. Some pieces of colored glass are also painted or etched to achieve pictorial details. The pieces of glass that make up a window are bound together by interlocking grooved lead strips, soldered at the joints and strengthened by iron cross supports. The window is then incorporated into a structure, becoming an integral part of an architectural whole.

This chapter is intended to give the reader a brief, general idea about how stained glass was made at the Keck Studio. The making of stained glass windows involved many steps, each requiring hand skills that took years of experience to master.

The Keck Studio was a business *(Figure 7)*. Its success depended on

Figure 6.   Men at work in Keck Studio shop, Syracuse, New York. Photo, 1928.
Keck Archives.

its profitable operation. In addition to designing windows, its directors, Henry Keck and, later, Stanley Worden, devoted much time to the routine chores of running an office (aided only by a secretary) and supervising a shop. The director also spent a good deal of time in promotion and sales. He advertised in such leading religious journals as *Church Management* as well as in local newspapers and directories. He exhibited at architectural conferences. Dwight Simmons, Keck's salesman for many years, traveled around the country calling on architects and church officials. Keck and Worden made similar calls when they traveled to Studio jobs. Clients often sought out the Studio on the basis of its reputation for quality work. The Studio sometimes entered and won competitions. Many prospective clients had little understanding of design process. Some assumed that stained glass windows were available ready-made. This was not the case; all windows were individually commissioned.

Some of the Studio's windows were for private residences or other secular buildings, but most of its large works were of sacred subjects and were installed in religious buildings of all denominations. Nearly all of these were for Catholic and Protestant churches. Since Jewish religious law prohibits portrayal of images in the temple, there was less call for stained glass windows in synagogues; even so, the studio executed a number of outstanding windows for social halls, schools, and other parts of synagogue buildings (*Figure 5*).

The means of determining subjects for windows varied according to religious faith. Before the 1960s, nearly all the decisions for Roman Catholic churches were made by a single person, either the bishop or the parish priest, though the donor of the window might indicate his preference for a subject. Protestant churches (and the more liberal Catholic parishes after 1960) typically depended on committees to choose window designs, invariably guided by their pastors. In Jewish congregations the rabbis usually decided, sometimes guided by committees. Only rarely did planning of sacred windows proceed along lines that stained glass studios considered ideal: determination of subjects, their treatment, and their placement made in concert by the architect of the building, the clergy, and informed and sensitive donors, all calling on the wisdom of the director of the stained glass studio and his artists. Typically, windows were added to a building almost as an afterthought, frequently over a period of many years as the parish could afford them and often by more than one studio.

As soon as a potential client contacted the Keck Studio, either with specific ideas for windows or with none at all, the director needed to know certain basic requirements in order to proceed with a design proposal. He

Figure 7.   Henry Keck and secretary in front office at 1010 West Genesee Street, Syracuse, the Studio's home after 1924. Photo, 1928. Keck Archives.

needed to ascertain the size and shape of the window openings, the sum available for the job, the subjects or themes for the windows, the architectural style of the building, its orientation to sources of light, and the desired level of interior lighting. Whenever possible, a member of the Studio staff visited the site.

Having obtained this information, a Studio artist selected from his files several watercolor designs (called *sketches*) for windows of similar requirements that the Studio had already made *(Figure 8)*. These were shown to the client to convey an impression of the color, light, and style that the Studio had used for equivalent commissions. Based on the client's response to these suggestions, the Studio sent a cost estimate. If the estimate was accepted, the staff began work on the project. At this point, if it had not already been done, the Studio sent a craftsman to the site to obtain exact measurements of the actual window opening(s) and to make templates (patterns) on cardboard or paper.

With an idea of the kind of design and style wanted, with the subject matter established, and with precise measurements to go by, the artist set out to create an original, detailed small scale (usually one inch to the foot) watercolor sketch for each window *(Figure 9)*. This presentation drawing was submitted to the client for final approval. These sketches were in nearly every case highly finished miniature paintings, matted in board cut to the shape of the window opening *(Plates 3 and 9)*. The sketch remained the property of the Studio.

Once approval was obtained, the artist prepared a full-sized drawing, called a *cartoon,* on heavy paper *(Figure 10)*. In this the artist developed the details of the watercolor sketch. In the early years of the Studio the making of this enlargement was a tedious and time-consuming process in which the cartoon was made full-scale freehand with the aid of grids. Beginning in the 1940s Worden greatly simplified this process with the use of an overhead projector to make the enlargement, tracing the major outlines from the projected image and then finishing the cartoon by adding inner lines, lead lines, shading, and details by eye with a brush and black ink or with charcoal. Once in a while the cartoon was colored with inks or pastels.

It was then necessary to make two copies of the cartoon. To do this, the artist (or an assistant) placed two sheets of heavy manila paper separated by carbon paper under the cartoon and traced the lines representing the shapes of each piece of glass (lead lines) with a stylus *(Figure 11)*. This made the *outline* and *pattern drawings*. All the sections of both drawings were identically numbered. To preserve the cartoon, the outline drawing was used in its stead as a master working drawing. It served as a guide for the place-

Figure 8. Studio artists Ernest Ashcroft (left) and Stanley Worden selecting watercolor sketches for a prospective client. Photo, 1967. Dick Bandy.

Figure 9.   Artist Ernest Ashcroft prepares watercolor sketch. Photo, 1967. Dick Bandy.

ment and binding with lead of the many pieces of glass and was eventually thrown away.

The other carbon copy, the pattern drawing, was cut up into pieces along its lead lines with either pattern scissors or a pattern knife. These tools have double blades or cutting edges to remove a narrow strip of paper (1/16 inch thick), thus providing the space needed between pieces of glass for the core of the grooved lead.

The artist then selected colors of glass for each piece of the window *(Plate 14)*. The Studio's glass came from a number of manufacturers, both in America and Europe. The Keck Studio usually had on hand well over five hundred different choices of glass in a wide range of colors, textures, thicknesses, and quality. Some were milky (opalescent), some clear; some were flat, some seeded, hammered, or wavy. There were at least fifty choices of blue glasses alone. Glass was not selected only on the basis of color and texture. Some was streaky and had to be oriented to represent folds in drapery or other visual effects (see Chapter 3 for a discussion of glass types).

Small numbered rectangles of each color sample were kept for reference in metal racks hung in the windows. Using the watercolor sketch as a guide, a studio artist selected colors for every pattern piece, noting its number on the outline drawing. Because the success of the entire window depended greatly upon color relationships, selecting glass was a highly specialized skill.

Large sheets of glass corresponding to the numbered samples were stored vertically in the studio glass racks *(Figure 12)*. Once selected, the sheets were pulled from stock and the glass cutter set to work. At this point the operation moved from the art department to the shop. Using the notations on the outline drawing and the numbered patterns to guide him, the craftsman cut each piece of glass according to the artist's color selection *(Figure 13)*. He used a common glass cutting tool equipped with a diamond, or preferably a steel wheel. This tool, a product of the late nineteenth century, is one of the new modern technical innovations in the craft. It allows for more rapid and exact glass cutting than did earlier methods. The craftsman then refined the cut edges of glass with a *grozing iron*, a tool with clawlike nippers used like a pair of pliers.

As the craftsman cut each piece of glass, he placed it in its proper place on the outline drawing *(Figure 14)*. When all of the pieces were cut, they were washed and dried. The window was then handed over to the *glazier* to be assembled unless it required glass painting. If so, the artist placed the pieces of glass onto the cartoon and traced the major linear

Figure 10.   Artists Stanley Worden (left) and Thomas Porter drawing full-sized cartoons for windows in St. Joseph's Chapel, Most Holy Rosary Catholic Church, Syracuse, New York. Photo, 1928. Keck Archives.

Figure 11. Office Manager Margaret Shepard assists tracing patterns. Ernest Ashcroft (left) and Stanley Worden in background. Photo, 1967. Dick Bandy.

Figure 12. Craftsman William Yost removing glass from glass racks. Photo, 1967.
Dick Bandy.

elements, called *trace lines,* onto the glass, painting them with a special vitrifiable *tracing color* made up of iron oxide, ground glass, gum arabic, and water. These pieces were laid on shallow trays and fired in a kiln to 1200° Fahrenheit, fusing the color to the glass. The artist could then proceed with the fine detailed painting without disturbing the trace lines. Because of unexplainable conditions due to weather, this intermediate firing was not usually necessary in summer months.

For the fine painting of details, the pieces of glass were fixed onto a moveable wood-framed, heavy plate glass easel (sash) *(Figure 15)*. Using the outline drawing as a guide, melted beeswax mixed with resin was dropped at the junction points of the glass pieces, sticking them to the glass sash on which they rested *(Figure 16)*. Spaces were left between the pieces to indicate the lead lines. Transluscent white paper was spread over the back of the easel to diffuse incoming light and the waxed-up window was suspended in strong natural light for painting.

Glass painting techniques are highly individual and vary according to the job. But most Keck Studio artists followed a procedure like that of Stanley Worden which is described here. First, everything not to be painted was blocked out (matted). This concentrated light on areas to be painted. With the exception of the use of *silver stain* applied to the back of glass to produce a yellow tone, the only other pigments the artist used were glass or *shading colors,* usually commercially prepared pigments of a reddish brown or black hue which were mixed with water on a palette. The artist brushed the shading colors evenly over the window in a thin coat, sometime stippling the surface to give it a texture. With a series of brushes and other tools, many of them handmade, Worden achieved the desired effects of shading and highlighting, detailing of faces, hands and feet, and modeling of drapery and other background features by carefully removing the shading color from areas where he wished the light to come through. This is the reverse of oil painting techniques wherein colors are added to create desired effects of light and shadow *(Figure 17)*.

When the painting was completed, the glass pieces were gently removed from the easel and the wax was scraped off. The pieces were refired. First they were placed in a warming-up chamber at the top of the kiln. One by one the steel plates on which they rested were moved with a specially designed fork into the firing chamber of the kiln which has been preheated to 1200° Fahrenheit. They were fired for about five minutes or until the glass colors melted (observed by eye) *(Figure 18)*, then quickly moved to the annealing oven where they were slowly cooled for about twenty-four hours, a process necessary to make the glass less brittle and more durable. The

Figure 13.   Shop foreman Hans Brand selecting and cutting glass. Photo, 1947.
Keck Archives.

Figure 14. Craftsman Harry McClean cutting and fitting glass to patterns. Photo, 1967.
Dick Bandy.

Figure 15.   Apprentice craftsman Daniel Shaw (left) and shop foreman Hans Brand
transferring cut glass to easel. Photo, 1947. Keck Archives.

Figure 16. Apprentice Daniel Shaw waxing glass to easel. Photo, 1947. Keck Archives.

Keck Studio was equipped with two German glass kilns with annealers and one muffle kiln, all fired with natural gas *(Figure 19)*.

The glass pieces were now ready for the *glazier (Figure 20)*. The outline drawing was fastened to his bench. Glazing lath was nailed down along two edges of the drawing to form a right angle against which the window would be assembled. The outside lead of the window was fastened inside the lath to form the edge of the window proper. The glazier cut pieces of grooved lead strips, called *cames,* which are soft and pliable and can be bent easily to fit around the lines of the design. From his beginning in one corner, the glazier assembled the pieces of glass, fitting each into cames. He cut the interlocking cames with a lead knife to match precisely the boundaries between pieces of glass. The window was assembled piece by piece like a jigsaw puzzle, the glazier tacking the cames in place with small nails until the next piece of glass was put into position.

When glazing was completed, all the joints were soldered *(Figure 21)*. The development of the electric soldering iron in the early twentieth century gave a tremendous advantage to modern stained glass craftsmen. Their predecessors used charcoal braziers to heat the irons.

To protect a window from the onslaught of the seasons—sun, snow, rain, wind, and worse—waterproofing cement was brushed into and around the cames on both sides of the window. Shop craftsmen then fixed metal reinforcing bars (flat, square, or round) to the window to keep it from buckling. Thus prepared, a window was capable of surviving for a century or more with a minimum of care *(Figure 22)*.

The finished window was set up in the Studio for inspection by the director or head artist. At this point, he might order the removal, darkening, lightening, or realigning of any piece of glass that did not enhance the overall effect of the finished window. It was this final judgment on which the Studio's reputation depended *(Figure 23)*. After any readjustments, the window was ready to be packed in heavy wooden boxes and shipped, usually by rail or motor freight, to the site of the installation. For local sites, the windows were hand delivered *(Figure 24)*.

Keck always sent his own glaziers to install the windows. The openings were usually prepared in advance by local builders. If it was a large window and T-bars were required, they were properly set into the opening frame by Keck's craftsmen. The window opening might be framed with stone, masonry, wood, steel, or aluminum; it might be three or thirty feet high; it might be at ground level or high in the air. All these variables required not only skills but sometimes also courage on the part of Keck craftsmen until the last panel was installed *(Figure 25)*.

Figure 17. Stanley Worden painting *Christ Blessing Children* window for St. Francis Xavier Catholic Church, Marcellus, New York. Photo, 1947. Keck Archives.

Figure 18.   Craftsman Werner Schultz at the firing chamber of the kiln. Photo, 1967.
Dick Bandy.

Figure 19. Craftsman Harry Chamberlain firing one of the Studio kilns. Photo, 1928.
Keck Archives.

Figure 20.   Craftsman William Yost lead glazing window. Photo, 1947. Keck Archives.

Figure 21.   Craftsman Robert Steinmiller soldering window. Photo, 1947. Keck Archives.

Figure 22.   Apprentice Daniel Shaw waterproofing windows. Photo, 1947. Keck Archives.

Figure 23. Henry Keck inspecting finished window. Photo, 1947. Keck Archives.

Figure 24.   Craftsman William Yost carries finished window out of the Keck Studio.
Photo, 1967. Dick Bandy.

Figure 25. Keck Studio craftsman installs window at St. Brigid's Catholic Church, Syracuse, New York. Photo, 1960. Stanley Worden.

The business manager recorded the time spent on each stage of the window's design and fabrication. The number of employees who worked on a window varied, but every window was a collaboration of artist and craftsman within the shop. Although each member of the Studio staff excelled in one or another phase of the process of making stained glass windows (selecting glass, glazing, etc.), most of them could perform all the procedures of their department. The head artist and the shop foreman constituted the minimum necessary staff to make a window, and in lean times, they were the only staff available. In better times, a small group of four to eight participated in the making of a window, several of them working in the art department or the front office. All of them, men and women alike, found in the Keck Studio the realization of its founder's aims that the highest standards of craft, art, and business practice would prevail in his domain.

3

American Neo-Gothic Stained Glass

HELEN JACKSON ZAKIN

EW YORK STATE is particularly blessed with a wealth of nine-teenth- and twentieth-century stained glass windows made by domestic and foreign artists and studios. New York City has the most concentrated collection of important windows, but beautiful stained glass can also be found in many upstate cities, towns, and villages.[1] St. Peter's Church in Albany has windows by several important English designers including Henry Holiday and Edward Burne-Jones. There are windows by John La Farge at Wells College in Au-rora, and Trinity Church in Buffalo. Tiffany windows can be seen all over the state: the 1910 list prepared by the Tiffany Studio listed more than 135 towns in New York State with buildings containing Tiffany windows.[2] In addition, there are many windows in this state by such well-known artists as Charles Connick, William Willet, and John Gordon Guthrie.

The smaller studios founded in Syracuse, Rochester, and Utica are less famous but just as important. The Henry Keck Studio, in particular, has supplied windows for many nearby and distant buildings and has had an important impact on the development of American stained glass.

Some of the earliest American windows are those dated 1847 at the Church of St. Ann and the Holy Trinity in Brooklyn, designed by William Bolton, who also made the windows for the Church of the Holy Apostles in Manhattan.[3] Many windows installed in American buildings in the third quarter of the nineteenth century were imported from England and Germany or made by American designers who had been influenced by English and German work. The Americans did not develop a distinctive style until the late 1870s when Tiffany and La Farge revolutionized the medieval craft of stained glass window making.

Louis Comfort Tiffany has always been credited with many of the technical innovations which characterized his work, but recent research indicated that John La Farge was the first to use opalescent glass and perhaps the first American glass designer to use plating.[4] Opalescent glass, which is cloudy, streaky, and sometimes iridescent, and plating (two or more layers of glass leaded together) made possible some of the daring aesthetic effects achieved by these two artists. Other innovations included drapery glass (crinkled when hot to suggest folded cloth) and copper foil (used instead of lead to bind the glass together) and chunks of glass called jewels.

Tiffany and La Farge, like their Pre-Raphaelite counterparts in England, had been trained as painters and both were very knowledgeable about the history of art. Much of their early work was influenced by Renaissance paintings. La Farge's axial window in Trinity Church, Buffalo, for example, is based on Giovanni Bellini's *Transfiguration of Christ*.[5] The design of a Tiffany aisle window in the same church is borrowed from a Raphael painting of St. Cecilia.[6] The Tiffany Studio, however, quickly developed a distinctive style, particularly associated with the designer Frederick Wilson, who was English trained. Wilson's use of lead to complement the drapery patterns, of diffused light, and of harmoniously arranged groups of figures resulted in stunning effects.

Opalescent windows were popular through the teens, but by the twenties new influences were coming to the fore. The major force behind the changes was Ralph Adams Cram, one of the most important church architects in the early twentieth century. Cram, a Neo-Gothic architect, had a very academic approach to medieval architecture and was highly critical of the stained glass styles developed under the aegis of La Farge and Tiffany. Cram particularly disapproved of Tiffany's three-dimensional landscape effects which he thought were inappropriate for stained glass, a medium which he thought should be decorative, two-dimensional, and subservient to the architecture. He expressed his opinions this way:

> A stained glass window is simply a piece of colored and translucent decoration, absolutely subordinate to its architectural environment, and simply a small component of a great artistic whole. It must continue the structural wall surface perfectly: therefore, it must be flat, without perspective or modelling. It must be decorative and conventional in design and color and in no respect naturalistic. It must never be a hole in a masonry wall, but a portion of that wall made transparent. It must not assert itself; that is, it must hold its place without insolence or insistence. It must be content to be just a means to an end,—no more.[7]

Cram wanted to revive the medieval glass designs, and in order to do that he encouraged and supported the work of William Willet and Charles Connick, among others.

The Neo-Gothic school was inspired by the twelfth- and thirteenth-century windows of European cathedrals, especially Chartres, which has held a special place in the American imagination since the appearance of Henry Adams' *Mont-Saint-Michel and Chartres* in 1913.[8] Henry Adams was a close friend of John La Farge, who had visited France on many occasions and who knew the Chartres glass well. It has even been suggested that Adams' comments on the Chartres glass are essentially based on La Farge's ideas.[9] The more liberal interpretation of the medieval aesthetic in the La Farge windows, however, did not suit Cram's taste; and it was Cram who wrote the introduction for Adams' 1913 edition, which was sponsored by the American Institute of Architects.

Thus Willet and Connick adopted medieval glazing models and, from their studios in Philadelphia and Boston, respectively, had a significant impact on the development of American glass. The Keck Studio was influenced by the work of both of these designers, but particularly by Connick.

Henry Keck, who designed some of the first windows produced by his Studio, had served as an apprentice in the Tiffany Studio. His expertise in using opalescent glass is evident in windows in St. Mary's Church, Mexico, New York *(Plates 2 and 15)*, and St. Patrick's Church, Johnstown, New York. His figures are softly idealized with rather heavily enameled faces.

Stanley Worden took over as chief designer at the Keck Studio in 1929 after he had served as an apprentice there since 1922. Worden had been trained to draw by Keck himself, and he also attended night classes in life drawing at Syracuse University from about 1926 until 1932. The strongest single influence on his work, however, were the windows designed by Charles Connick.[10] Worden saw Connick windows in New York and Boston, among other places, and was familiar with his work through *Stained Glass,* the publication of the Stained Glass Association of America. From 1933 to 1948 the magazine was edited by Orin Skinner, Connick's colleague in the Boston studio and chief designer there after Connick's death. Worden had also seen Connick's very influential book, *Adventures in Light and Color,* published in 1937.

In addition to the work of Charles Connick, the Keck designers were also influenced by Arts and Crafts magazines such as *International Studio,* books of ornament, and published prints of religious paintings. Prints of the work of the German artist Bernhard Plockhorst had a particular influence on the work of Thomas Porter. Worden also used ornament books for reference, especially Alexander Speltz's *Styles of Ornament Exhibited in Designs* and *Kunsthistorischen Bildenbogen fur den Gebrauch bei Akademischen,* a book of reproductions of tracery patterns, canopy patterns, figural designs, and metalwork published in Leipzig in 1883 and presumably brought back by Keck after his training in Munich. Worden never copied these images, but rather adapted them for specific commissions. The canopy work in the windows at St. Joseph's Catholic Church, Dannemora, New York, designed by Worden in 1931 and 1942, represents a free adaptation of published designs.

Worden and the other designers who worked for Keck were a part of the Gothic movement in American stained glass. Worden's designs for St. Mary's Church in Amsterdam, New York (1941–1948) *(Figure 30, Plates 11 and 16),* Gobin Memorial Methodist Church at De Pauw University, Greencastle, Indiana (1940s–1970) *(Figures 26 and 27),* Church of the Ascension, Rochester, New York (1946) *(Plate 10),* and St. Paul's Episcopal Church, Endicott, New York (1956, 1968), show this medievalizing influence in the use of twelfth- and thirteenth-century ornament and architectural canopies, a predominantly red-blue color balance, elongated figures, and Neo-Gothic drapery. The pose and gesture of the *Sower* figure in the window in the Gobin Church, for example, are based on the popular and often-copied Millet painting, but the drapery has been rendered in an early thirteenth-century style that is derived from Mosan metalwork. The Madonna and Child in the center lancet of this multilight window are framed by a colored architectural canopy that is reminiscent of thirteenth-century Gothic windows. The figure is placed on a deep blue ground, against which red stars sparkle. The blue ground is broken up by random lead lines and blue glasses of slightly different hues have been used to suggest the effect of hand-blown medieval pot metal. The term *pot metal* refers to glass colored in the molten state with metallic oxides. Pot metal was characteristically all one color—though it was made in small quantities and every batch was different—and comparatively thin. Two types of glass were generally used in twentieth-century Neo-Gothic windows: antique glass and cathedral glass. *Antique glass* was introduced to the United States in the early 1920s from Europe by the Blenko Glass Company of Milton, West Virginia. It is hand-blown into cylinders and then flattened into 18 × 24 inch sheets. It is full of bubbles and appears variegated in color, even though it is not, because of its uneven thickness (from 1/16 to 3/8 inch thick). A variation is *flashed glass* in which a layer of colored glass is annealed to a layer of clear glass. Antique glass was an attempt to imitate pot metal. *Cathedral glass,* on the other hand, is machine rolled rather than hand-blown. It is produced in large sheets (32 × 84 inches) of even thickness, which are often given surface textures (double-rolled, seedy, ripple, etc.) and is much cheaper to make and use.

The Neo-Gothic style dominated American stained glass in the twenties, thirties, and forties and influenced it even into the fifties: most of the major American studios and designers worked in this mode. Besides Keck, Connick, and Willet, one could mention Lamb (New York), Burnham (Boston), D'Ascenzo (Philadelphia), Lakeman (New York), Reynolds, Francis & Rohnstock (Boston), Bonawit (New York), Goodhue (New York), Young (New York), and Guthrie (New York). Neo-Gothic stained glass was commissioned to fill the hundreds of large windows in Neo-Gothic churches. Trinity Episcopal Church in Syracuse, for example, has a north wall World War I memorial window by William Willet (1919) and three aisle windows by the Henry Wynd Young Studio (1926–1929). The remaining aisle windows were made by the Keck Studio between 1947 and 1949. Worden succeeded in designing windows which resemble but do not copy the Young ones, and the resulting effect is harmonious (*Figures 28 and 29*).

Not all twentieth-century windows were designed in the Neo-Gothic style. The windows of Frank Lloyd Wright, George Grant Elmslie, and other Prairie School architects represent a different aspect of twentieth-century glass. Wright's designs are not related to the opalescent windows of Tiffany and La Farge, with their figural and landscape imagery, or to Neo-Gothic windows. Rather, Wright's windows, such as those designed for the Dana-Thomas House in Springfield, Illinois (1903), are characterized by straight lead lines, a preponderance of white glass with pale brown and yellow touches, and geometric patterns.[11] The basic motif is said to be a stylized sumac plant. The Avery Coonley playhouse windows by Wright (1912), now in the Metropolitan Museum of Art, New York, are based on a balloon motif, using bits of bright red, blue, and green glass, but the basic lines are verticals and horizontals, and most of the windows are clear glass, as are the Elmslie windows in the Metropolitan Museum (1911).[12] The windows designed by Wright and Elmslie are related to those of Louis Sullivan.[13] These in turn may be somewhat indebted to the window designs of Frank Furness.[14] Wright was employed as a draftsman and shop foreman in Chicago by Sullivan who had worked for Furness in Philadelphia.

In the fifties and sixties American stained glass styles changed dramatically as a result of the movement in modern painting toward abstraction, and also as a result of innovations in stained glass technology. European glaziers developed a new technique known as *dalles de verre* which consisted of thick glass slabs set into epoxy resin producing effects of

61

Figure 26. *Nativity.* Seven-lancet, Neo-Gothic antique glass window for Gobin Memorial Methodist Church, DePauw University, Greencastle, Indiana. Designed and painted by Stanley Worden. 1947. Photo, 1983. Heila Martin.

Worden designed all the windows for this church. The subjects of this window are, on the left, *The Boy Christ in the Temple* and *Christ Preaching in the Synagogue*; in the center, the three-panel *Nativity*; and on the right, the *Parables* of *The Sower* and *The Good Samaritan*.

Figure 27.   Parable of the Sower. Detail of antique glass window in Gobin Memorial Methodist Church *(Figure 26)*, DePauw University, Greencastle, Indiana. Designed and painted by Stanley Worden. 1947. Photo, 1983. Heila Martin.

Figure 28.   St. James and St. Thomas. One of a series of antique glass nave windows, 82 x 22 inches, for Trinity Episcopal Church, Syracuse, New York. Designed and painted by Stanley Worden. 1949. Photo, 1982. Cleota Reed. These windows were made to complement windows made for the church in 1929 by the Henry Wynd Young Studio of New York City *(see Figure 29).*

Figure 29.   St. Joel and St. Hosea. One of a series of nave windows designed by the Henry Wynd Young Studio of New York City for Trinity Episcopal Church, Syracuse, New York in 1929. Photo, Keck Archives.

deep color. The Europeans were probably also largely responsible for the adoption of abstract imagery since there had been a great revival of stained glass in Europe following World War II because of the pressing need to replace windows which had been destroyed. These new European techniques and modern imagery quickly reached upstate New York. There are some striking *dalles de verre* windows in the Fulton United Methodist Church (1964) designed and installed by the Willet Studio. Ronald Shaw designed windows of "dallies" or faceted glass, as it was known in the trade, made for the Methodist Church in Vestal, New York, in 1961 by the Keck Studio.

Clearly, stained glass technology has evolved in partnership with stained glass design. The stylistic changes reflect a general evolution visible also in painting, sculpture, and the decorative arts, but stained glass also serves a particular architectural function. The development of architectural styles, specifically church architecture, has had an important impact on glass imagery. In most cases, buildings are finished before the glass is designed. Frequently the architect selects the stained glass artist who must make the window imagery conform to the architecture. Stanley Worden designed the *Revelations* window for the First Presbyterian Church in Van Wert, Ohio, to fit the complicated stone tracery which had already been installed.

Nineteenth- and twentieth-century stained glass evinces creativity second only to the windows of the medieval period and many of the most interesting nineteenth- and twentieth-century windows were made in America, yet the history of American stained glass has never been written, and research on the subject is still in its infancy. Louis Comfort Tiffany, the most famous American stained glass personality, has been the subject of many books and articles, and some research has been done on the windows of John La Farge, Tiffany's less well-known contemporary. Until recently, however, scholars and critics had published little else about American stained glass artists and studios.

In general, the most active periods in the development of American glass have been periods of economic growth and prosperity—the late nineteenth and early twentieth centuries, the 1920s, the 1940s, and the 1950s. The subjects of many of these windows reflect specific concerns, as for example, World War memorials. In many cases, ambitious nineteenth-century buildings with elaborate windows were constructed in communities which have ceased to prosper; however, these monuments remind us of earlier values, traditions, and ideals too valuable to ignore. Once lost they can never be replaced and another tool for understanding our past is gone.

NOTES

1. James Sturm, *Stained Glass from Medieval Times to the Present: Treasures to be Seen in New York* (New York: Dutton, 1982).

2. Tiffany Studios, *A Partial List of Windows* (New York: Tiffany Studios, 1910; 2nd printing, Watertown, Mass.: John H. Sweeny, 1972.)

3. Willene B. Clark, "America's First Stained Glass: William Jay Bolton's Windows at the Church of the Holy Trinity, Brooklyn, New York," *American Art Journal* 11 (1979): 32–53.

4. The latest publications on Tiffany include: Hugh McKean, *The Lost Treasures of Louis Comfort Tiffany* (New York: Doubleday, 1980), and Alastair Duncan, *Tiffany Windows* (New York: Simon and Schuster, 1980). See also James Sturm, "Louis Comfort Tiffany: His Windows and his World," *Stained Glass* 76 (1981–82): 323–28. For John La Farge see H. Barbara Weinberg, *The Decorative Work of John La Farge* (New York: Garland Press, 1977), pp. 339–469; H. Barbara Weinberg, "John La Farge and the Invention of American Opalescent Windows," *Stained Glass* 67 (1972): 4–11; and Henry Adams, "The Stained Glass of John La Farge," *American Art Review* 2 (1975): 41–53.

5. Frederick Hartt, *History of Italian Renaissance Art,* 2d ed. (New York: Abrams, 1979), color plate 57

6. John Pope-Hennessy, *Raphael* (New York: Harper & Row, 1970), p. 231, fig. 217.

7. Ralph Adams Cram, *Church Building; a Study of the Principles of Architecture in their Relation to the Church* (Boston: Small, Maynard, & Co., 1901), p. 139.

8. The book was first privately printed by Adams in 1904 and then published in 1913.

9. Robert Mane, *Henry Adams on the Road to Chartres* (Cambridge: Belknap Press, 1971), p. 70.

10. Personal interview with Stanley Worden, 2 December 1982.

11. Richard R. Morse and Ralls Melotte, "The Dana-Thomas House," *Stained Glass* 77 (1982): 138–41, and Ralls C. Melotte and Richard R. Moore, "The Dana-Thomas House: Symbol of a Revolution," ibid. 265–68.

12. Sharon S. Darling, *Chicago Ceramics and Glass* (Chicago: Chicago Historical Society, 1979), p. 124, fig. 125.

13. See for example the stained glass in the National Farmer's Bank (1907–1908) illustrated in Frank Lloyd Wright, *Genius and the Mobocracy* (New York: Horizon Press, 1971), p. 223.

14. Art library, University of Pennsylvania, Philadelphia (1891) illustrated in James F. O'Gorman, *The Architecture of Frank Furness* (Philadelphia: Philadelphia Museum of Art, 1973), p. 170, fig. 29–15.

4

The Windows of St. Mary's Church

CLEOTA REED

s. Mary's Church in Amsterdam, New York, a small city about thirty miles northwest of Albany on the Mohawk River, has some of the most interesting Keck Studio stained glass windows in New York State. Four of the windows, all dating from the 1940s, are especially noteworthy for their unusual iconographic programs. One of these concerns the history of freedom, tracing it from Moses to modern America. Another concerns the place of worship in the lives of modern Americans of all walks of life. In both subject and design these two windows show an important kinship to the democratically oriented arts of mural painting and poster design of the 1930s and 1940s, with their emphasis on social realism. The other two windows are portraits of figures of major importance in the early history of Christianity in the Mohawk Valley.

The windows are the product of a collaboration between Father Edward A. Walsh (1880–1964), pastor of the church, and Stanley E. Worden, the Keck Studio designer who realized in stained glass the priest's program for the windows. Collaborations between clergymen and stained glass artists have always been common, but in this case Father Walsh's uncommonly adventurous imagination and Worden's sensitivity to the needs of the program created memorable results.

The collaboration began in 1941 when Father Walsh asked the Keck Studio to design a transom and eight doorlights for the parish rectory, a building dating from 1887. These incorporated standard Christian emblems. He also ordered two small circular windows for the church building itself, a structure erected in the late 1860s. The design for one of these round windows was adapted from Raphael's tondo, *The Madonna of the Chair* (Pitti Palace, Florence). Shortly afterward came two large figure windows, *Christ Triumphant* and *Christ in Gethsemane,* the latter after the popular Heinrich Hoffman image. Up to this point the program was conventional, and even rather old fashioned. The main distinction of the windows was the high quality of their execution.

But Father Walsh also ordered two windows to be placed high on the side walls of the transept and the subjects of these, *St. Isaac Jogues* and *Kateri Tekakwitha,* were far from old fashioned. We will return to them shortly. A year later, in 1942, he commissioned an *Immaculate Conception* window to rise above the high altar *(Figure 30)* and then, early in 1945, he ordered a war memorial window on the subject of *Liberty* for the west transept *(Plate 11)*. These two windows are the largest in the church as well as the most original in subject and the most striking in design. In 1947 Worden designed a *Supper at Emmaus* window for the east transept, which though more traditional in context was made in the style of the *Liberty,* as a companion piece. Finally, in 1948, he designed three smaller, traditional windows for the baptistry, *Christ and Nicodemus, Mary and the Child,* and *Baptism of Christ.* These are Neo-Gothic in style, characterized by rich color, intricate lead work, and fine painting.[1] They completed an unusual and varied program, unusual not only because of some of its subjects but also because a large part of it was executed during and immediately after the war when materials were scarce.

During the years that Worden was deeply involved in the designs for these windows, Father Walsh also commissioned the Keck Studio to restore the twelve existing nave windows, figures of the Apostles, made in the late 1890s by the Flanagan-Biedenweg Studio of Chicago. Keck craftsmen removed these windows and took them to Syracuse to repair the leads and restore the glass painting. To avoid the expense of taking the windows entirely apart, which would have been necessary to fire new true glass painting, the painted sections were superficially retouched with oil paints and varnished. Father Walsh apparently chose to stop short of full-scale restoration of this old glass because he knew that the church's new windows would draw heavily on his resources. Keck imported Adolph Rotenecker from New York to spruce up the Flanagan-Biedenweg windows.

Worden's two transept windows of St. Isaac Jogues and Kateri Tekakwitha depict a pair of sacred figures that had rarely, if ever, been portrayed in stained glass before, except in other upstate New York churches by the Keck Studio. Their presence in St. Mary's is quite natural, however, since in the seventeenth century the historical Jogues and Kateri were both

Figure 30.   Immaculate Conception. Watercolor sketch, 18¾ x 11¾ inches. Design for antique glass altar window for St. Mary's Catholic Church, Amsterdam, New York. Stanley Worden. 1942. Keck Archives.

associated with the region of the Mohawk River of which Amsterdam is now the major center of population.

The common association of Jogues and Kateri was with Ossernenon, a Mohawk village of the Turtle Clan of the Iroquois Confederacy. It stood on the south side of the Mohawk River, near present-day Auriesville, where a twentieth-century shrine commemorates the Jesuit Martyrs. At Ossernenon Jogues and Kateri, in different times and in different ways, performed the deeds that in the seventeenth century made them legendary figures and in the twentieth century caused one to be elevated to sainthood and the other to be beatified.

Isaac Jogues (1607–1646), a French Jesuit missionary in Canada, was one of the first Europeans to penetrate deeply into the American wilderness. In 1641 he gave Sault Sainte Marie, on Lake Superior, its name. In 1643, while returning to Quebec, he was captured, tortured, and held in slavery for more than a year in Ossernenon by the Iroquois before he was ransomed by the Dutch. When he returned to France he was "allowed by Pope Urban VIII the very exceptional privilege of celebrating Mass, which the mutilated condition of his hands had made canonically impossible. . . . He was called a martyr of Christ by the Pontiff. No similar concession, up to that, is known to have been granted."[2] In 1646, once again in North America, Jogues discovered Lake George and embarked on missions of peace with the Iroquois. His former captors at Ossernenon first received him well, but on his final visit the Iroquois, ravaged by sickness, seized him as a sorcerer and blamed him for their plight. He and his companion, Father Jean Lalande, were savagely murdered, and their bodies were thrown into the Mohawk River. Fathers Jogues and Lalande are two of the eight Jesuit Martyrs of North America.[3]

The Amsterdam window portrays Jogues as a saint in priestly robes, holding a crucifix. A rustic cross, symbolic of the early attempts to Christianize the Indians, is included in a medallion above his figure. His wounds are healed and his fingers restored in sainthood. In the popular prints of his own century, long before his canonization, these signs of martyrdom were vividly shown. The Jogues window, like its companion, the Kateri Tekakwitha window, is a modified Neo-Gothic design, with geometric grisaille-patterned background. The modifications are all in the direction of the streamlined style of American Scene realism of the 1930s and 1940s. In both windows the statuesque figures are placed in dark blue aureoles.

Kateri Tekakwitha (1656–1680), orphaned, scarred, and nearly blinded by smallpox as a small child, was raised by her uncle, a chief of the Turtle Clan at Ossernenon, her birthplace. Resisting marriages proposed for

Plate 9. *St. Michael and Twelve Virtues.* Watercolor sketch, 12 inches in diameter. Design for antique glass rose window for the First Presbyterian and Trinity Church, South Orange, New Jersey. Stanley Worden. 1948. Keck Archives. Photo, 1982. Courtney Frisse.

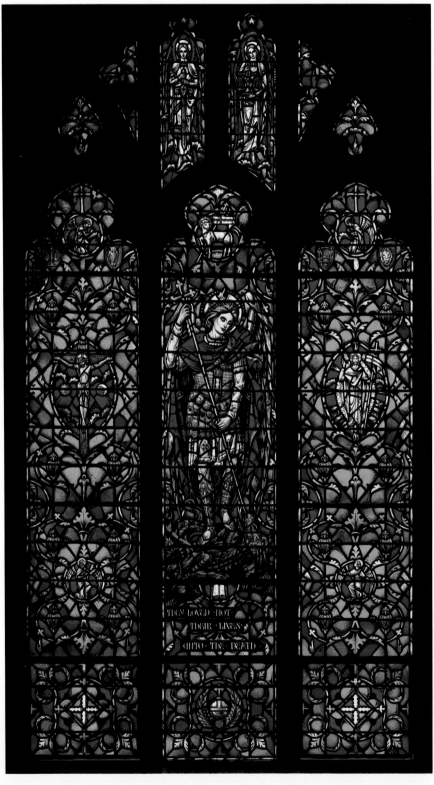

Plate 10. *St. Michael.* Painted antique glass window, 15 x 8 feet, for Episcopal Church of the Ascension, Rochester, New York. Designed and painted by Stanley Worden. 1945. Photo, 1982. Courtney Frisse.

Plate 11. Liberty. Painted antique glass window, 15 x 9 feet, for St. Mary's Catholic Church, Amsterdam, New York. Designed and painted by Stanley Worden. 1945. Photo, 1982. Courtney Frisse.

Plate 12. Emblem of the State of New York, Dewitt Clinton and Peter Minuit. Painted, combination antique and opalescent window, 10 x 7 feet, for Assembly Chamber lobby, New York State Capitol, Albany. Designed by David Lithgow, and painted and executed by Henry Keck. 1950. Photo, 1982. Courtney Frisse. Keck returned to the older opalescent style to make this window harmonize with the late nineteenth-century style of the Capitol.

Plate 13. *Flight into Egypt.* Painted antique stained glass window, 13½ x 5 feet. One of a series of nave windows for the Church of the Transfiguration, Syracuse, New York. Designed by Stanley Worden and painted by Worden and Ronald Shaw. 1956. Photo, 1982. Courtney Frisse.

Plate 14.   Stanley Worden Selecting Glass. Photo, 1967. Dick Bandy.

Plate 15. *Kateri Tekakwitha.* Painted antique glass figure window, 8 x 2¾ feet, for St. Mary's Roman Catholic Church, Mexico, New York. Designed and painted by Stanley Worden. 1944. Photo, 1982. Courtney Frisse.

Plate 16. *Kneeling Indian.* Detail of *Immaculate Conception* window *(Figure 30)*, St. Mary's Roman Catholic Church, Amsterdam, New York. Designed and painted by Stanley Worden. 1942. Photo, 1983. Cleota Reed.

her, she vowed to become a Christian and to live a life of exemplary holiness. In spite of strong opposition from her family, she was baptized at age eighteen by Father Jacques de Lamberville in the Mohawk Castle (village) of Caughnawaga, near present-day Fonda, just north of the Mohawk River.[4] Her baptism reportedly caused a wave of conversion to Christianity within the Indian community. Because of opposition from tribal heads, she was advised to move to Canada and walked two hundred miles to Sault Saint Louis near Montreal in October 1677. In 1680 she died at the Caughnawaga Mission in Quebec at age twenty-four. The story of her exemplary life was told and retold throughout Europe. She has come to be known variously as the "Mohawk Virgin," "the Lily of the Mohawk," and "Genevieve of New France."[5] Her brief life was one of remarkable austerity, charity, and sanctity.

Worden's Amsterdam figure of Kateri (as well as others he designed for a number of New York State churches over the years), derives from romantic prints of the late nineteenth and early twentieth centuries. These have no connection with the only contemporary likeness of Kateri, which is the portrait drawn from memory by Claude Chauchetiere who had met Kateri in Quebec. An engraving after Chauchetiere was published in 1717, thirty-seven years after her death. This shows a standing, veiled Kateri carrying a small crucifix in one hand while holding the other hand against her breast. Her eyes are closed, suggesting both prayerful meditation and her virtual blindness. Her face is pockmarked. Later, romanticized popular images of Kateri uncover her head, open her eyes, smooth her complexion, and place her next to a large rustic cross.

It is this romantic image that Worden adapted and freely transformed for his window. Kateri's costume is largely one of drapery, making it consistent with the biblical robes of the Apostles in the nave and the priestly robes of St. Isaac Jogues in the opposing transept. She wears trousers and moccasins under her robes. In this regard Worden is in tune with Chauchetiere who also showed trousered legs extending below a long tunic. Worden places her by a rustic cross. Her hands are clasped as in prayer. In a medallion in the upper part of the window, a tomahawk crosses an axe, symbolizing the union of American Indian and European cultures in the wilderness.

In the early 1930s both Father Isaac Jogues and Kateri Tekakwitha were the subjects of much attention in New York State. In 1930 the martyred priest was elevated to sainthood. In 1932 Kateri became the first American Indian candidate for sainthood. At this point they began to appear in glass. The Keck Studio's earliest portrayal of them was in a pair of windows designed by Thomas Porter for St. Cecilia's Roman Catholic Church in Fonda, a parish embracing both the place of Kateri's baptism and the presumed site of the murder of Jogues and Lalande. In 1933, Bishop Edmund F. Gibbons of the Albany Diocese donated a Kateri Tekakwitha window, commissioned from the Keck Studio by Father Anthony Krugler for his parish's Church of the Resurrection in Germantown, New York, on the Hudson River some thirty miles below Albany. (There is no Jogues window in this church). Father Walsh's windows were therefore at least the third instance in the Albany Diocese in which one or both of the Jogues and Kateri subjects appeared in stained glass in a church. Bishop Gibbons had himself introduced Kateri as a candidate for sainthood in Rome.

In 1957 Worden designed Jogues and Kateri windows for St. Mary's Roman Catholic Church in Mexico, New York *(Plate 15)*. The figures in this pair are very much like the ones in Amsterdam. He also depicted Kateri, along with all eight of the Jesuit Martyrs, on a small scale in modern windows for the Jesuit Provincial House at LeMoyne College in Syracuse in 1966.

The next window for the St. Mary's program, the *Immaculate Conception* of 1942, is approximately twelve feet wide and eighteen feet high, far larger than the two figure windows *(Figure 30)*. The window is dedicated to the memory of all deceased priests and parishoners of the church. If the Jogues and Kateri windows were meant to call to mind the great figures of Christianity who in an earlier century had lived in the environs of Amsterdam, the *Immaculate Conception* window was meant to emphasize the centrality of Christian belief in modern, democratic American society as it was known in Amsterdam.

Father Walsh specified every detail of the window's iconography. Rising from the center within a mandorla, Mary on a crescent moon is attended by angels and cherubs. Beneath this traditional representation of the *Immaculate Conception* is an array of figures surprising in their variety. In naturalistic poses, they form the lower part of a circular design which is completed by an arc of angels in the sky. The landscape beneath the Virgin Mary contains a factory with smokestacks, a church, and houses, symbolic of industrial mid-twentieth-century Amsterdam.

The figures gathered worshipfully in the foreground include a kneeling Sister of Charity with her billowing white headdress and a seated, robed woman holding a child. On the right side of the window are figures of Moses, a bishop, a parish priest, Saint Isaac Jogues, and an American Indian in tribal dress *(Plate 16)*, an unconventional grouping that links Old and New Testaments, Judaism and Christianity, the white and red races, and higher and lower levels of priestly authority. Included are symbols of self sacrifice (Jogues), conversion (the kneeling Indian), law (Moses), authority (the bishop), and service (the priest). On the left are the "people," men and women of several walks of life: a physician, a surveyor, a professor, a statesman, a nurse, a laborer, and a farmer. It is rare that an American church window gives so much attention to worshipers, rarer still that it portrays worshipers so democratically. The *Immaculate Conception* window was a departure from the prevailing long-established practices of American window design that sought traditional subjects and historic styles for traditional buildings. Father Walsh's program emphasized the modernity of traditional worship, the broadness of Christianity's appeal, and its Old Testament roots. In both subject and style, the lower part of the window reminds the viewer of the WPA murals that were painted in countless post offices and other public buildings across the land. As public works the murals avoided overt references to religious subjects, except in the most innocuous ways. But Father Walsh put religious faith at the center of his program, while also drawing on the secular, social-realist symbolism of American artists of the era.

Father Walsh's beliefs also underlie the *Liberty* window of 1945, though they are expressed differently *(Plate 11)*. Fifteen feet high and nine feet wide, the window is a memorial to the American men and women who died in World War II. There was a rash of war memorial windows soon after both World Wars *(Figure 31)*. Some depicted soldiers in contemporary dress. Nearly all were highly patriotic. Many, like Worden's *St. Michael* windows in the Episcopal Church of the Ascension in Rochester *(Plate 10)* and in the First Presbyterian and Trinity Church in South Orange, New Jersey *(Plate 9)*, and Ronald Shaw's *St. Michael* window for the 82nd Airborne Chapel, Fort Bragg, North Carolina *(Figure 32)*, portray the archangel, clothed in a dazzling coat of mail with resplendent wings rising from his shoulders, slaying Satan in the guise of a dragon. The Archangel Michael, as the Protector of the Jewish nation and, after the Christian revelation, the Protector of the Church Militant in Christendom, was the single most popular subject for war memorials. But Father Walsh avoided what may have seemed to him to be too conventional a subject and devised one that was more complex and original. Rather than emphasizing victory, he took as his subject the history of liberty, the ideal for which the war had been fought. The window finds the origins and sustenance of liberty in the Judeo-Christian tradition, and its vital champions first in historical men and women and, finally, in the American people.

The window consists of three lancets, surmounted by two kite sections and a central triangle that together form a rounded top. In the upper

Figure 31.   Mass on World War I Battlefield. Watercolor sketch, 3½ inches square.
Design for antique glass war memorial window for St. Joseph's Catholic Church,
Middletown, New York. Stanley Worden. 1932. Keck Archives. Worden presented this
design for a small window, but the parish priest liked it so much that the subject was used
instead for a large nave window.

Figure 32. St. Michael. Watercolor, 16 x 12¼ inches. Design for antique glass World War II memorial narthex window for 82nd Airborne Chapel, Fort Bragg, North Carolina. Ronald Shaw. 1959. Keck Archives.

part of the central lancet is an ascending figure of Christ, hands raised, the linear vertical flow of his robes emphasized by arms upraised to embrace Heaven. Above his hands in the apex of the central lancet, is an image of God the Father, surmounted by a dove symbolic of the Holy Spirit. Beneath Christ is the motto "Where the spirit of God is, there is Liberty." These words of St. Paul form the leitmotif of the window. In the upper part of the left lancet, a figure of the Virgin Mary holding the Christ Child is titled "Queen of Peace." Four smaller female figures share her section of the lancet, each chosen by Father Walsh for her contribution to the history of freedom. These are Judith and Esther from the Old Testament and St. Joan of Arc and St. Catherine of Siena from the late Middle Ages. The first three are included as liberators of peoples from tyranny or foreign domination; St. Catherine is included as the liberator of the papacy from its exile in Avignon.

In the right lancet is a figure of "Moses Liberator," accompanied by four smaller male figures. These are the biblical David, the legendary St. George, Don Juan of Austria, and Christopher Columbus. As liberators, these are a distinctly varied foursome. Father Walsh justified their presence in his freedom window as follows:

> in David's case, for his conquest of the Philistines; St. George, for the story of his removal of the menace of the English dragon which authorities think was a symbolic reference to the legendary slaying of the monster Diocletian, cruel persecutor of Christian life and Christian teaching; Columbus, for the part he played, together with that of the early Catholic missionaries, in freeing the early American settlers from barbaric paganism and leading them in time into the freedom and light of the children of the true God; and who can ever hope to forget Don Juan and his dashing and decisive victory at Lepanto where, by his incredible ability and bravery, he stayed the mighty menace to European civilization and Christianity hurled at them by the fury and demonical hate of the Moslem hordes of Islam bent upon the despotic domination of the Christian world.[6]

This program occupies the upper two-thirds of the window. The lower and more strikingly original third carries the history of freedom, in the words of Father Walsh, "from the sphere of religious history, . . . investing it with a touch of sheer secular or profane significance." The design consists of two horizontal bands. The uppermost of these includes depictions of the signing of the Magna Carta by King John, traditionally the origin of the institution of liberty in the modern world, and the signing of the Declaration of Independence, the symbolic act that created an entire nation from the concept of liberty. The latter detail is an adaptation of John Trumbull's well-known painting, an image known to virtually all American school children. In showing the figures of Jefferson and Franklin in this detail, the window enlarges its reach to include deists and free-thinkers. In the center of that band, freed men of King John's England and an officer of the Continental Army (Washington?) kneel in prayer before the Lamb of God.

The lowermost section, closest to the viewer, is vividly described by Father Walsh as:

> A modern conception of the defense of liberty in the form of figures of various branches of our present day military service; on the one hand the marching Waves, Wacs, Nurses and Marines, while on the other may be seen the militant marching forms of soldiers, sailors, marines and fliers. These two panels in turn flank a central one which bears a reproduction of Isaiah's inspired reference to the era of peace to come when "swords would be turned into ploughshares and the lion come to lie down with the lamb."[7]

It matters little that Father Walsh made the common error of pairing Isaiah's lion with a lamb—the prophet actually specified wolf and lamb. More important is his notion that the proper place for a war memorial was in a setting, such as a church, that encouraged contemplation, and not, as he says, in "a public square or park . . . where commerce and seething life rush by in heedless and vulgar indifference." Yet in both his *Liberty* and *Immaculate Conception* windows he sought to direct meditation to present-day life and to the democratic, interdenominational, latitudinarian spirit that characterized the 1940s. The naturalism of Worden's figures in both windows serve this goal well.

In the *Liberty* window Worden unifies the remarkably diverse elements of the program with color, strong composition, a bold linear style, and a convincing naturalism that harmonizes the several styles of the details, from the Pre-Raphaelite flavor of the trumpeting angels in the kites through the Neo-Gothic Christ figure to the war bond poster style of the marching figures at the bottom of the window. The window is also unified by the tension of contrasting elements. A contemplative Mary balances an active Moses; one serenely presents the infant Jesus to the world while the other, with a grandly sweeping gesture, lays down the law to humanity. The band of inscriptions beneath the figures of Mary, Christ, and Moses not only divides the window into its sacred and secular parts but also acts as a unifying element, its style echoed in subsidiary inscriptions above and below.

Worden was a master of this kind of design and he was also a master of color. Blue dominates the window, as it does most Neo-Gothic work, suggesting other-worldliness, the heavens, and the ethereal spaces of eternity. Worden used some forty shades of blue hand-blown antique glass in the window. The variable thickness of the glass adds a variety of hue and intensity to each shade. Color directs attention to the gloriously golden eagle, adapted from the Great Seal of the United States of America. As a design element it is second in importance only to the head of Christ. Surmounting the peacefully coexisting lion and lamb, it proclaims America as the home of liberty.

With the passage of a generation, Father Walsh's program may seem somewhat simplistic and jingoistic. But in the mid-1940s it was, of course, right in line with deeply held beliefs in America. Further, the program was aimed not at highly sophisticated tastes but rather at a congregation consisting of many laborers, housewives, and others whose acquaintance with art and literature was meager. Nevertheless, compared to other expressions of the same ideas in posters, murals, and magazines, the *Liberty* window stands up very well indeed.[8]

In the originality of their concepts as well as in their execution, the *Liberty* and *Immaculate Conception* windows represent high achievement in the history of American stained glass. An imaginative pastor, a locale rich in history, an exceptionally able stained glass artist, an equally able shop of craftsmen, and a parish farsighted enough to preserve its treasures have made the Amsterdam windows among the most memorable accomplishments of the Henry Keck Stained Glass Studio.

NOTES

1. Specifications for the St. Mary's windows can be found in the Order Books of the Keck Studio Archives, Onondaga Historical Association, Syracuse, New York. Mr. Worden and Mrs. Margaret Habla, present secretary for St. Mary's Church, provided important details about Father Walsh and the church.

2. *Catholic Encyclopedia,* 1st ed. (1910), s.v. "Jogues."

3. Ibid.

4. Now listed on the National Register of Historic Places, this site was excavated by archeologists between 1950 and 1958. It is the only entire Iroquois Indian village that has been excavated in the United States and is on the property of the Tekakwitha Shrine, Fonda, New York.

5. *New Catholic Encyclopedia,* 1st ed. (1967), s.v. "Tekakwitha."

6. Father Edward Walsh, *Souvenir of the Dedication of the Liberty Memorial Window in St. Mary's Church, Amsterdam, N.Y.* (Amsterdam, 1945), 14 pp.

7. Ibid.

8. James Sturm, in his *Stained Glass from Medieval Times to the Present: Treasures to be Seen in New York* (New York: Dutton, 1982), p. 71, notes that attempts to transcend a medieval setting while retaining a distinctly medieval style are not always successful. "We squirm in a time warp," he says, "seeing a Gothic Abraham Lincoln deliver the Gettysburg Address." Worden's windows are notable for overcoming this problem.

Bibliographic Note

HE BEST INTRODUCTION to the history of American stained glass is James Sturm's *Stained Glass from Medieval Times to the Present: Treasures to be Seen in New York* (New York: Dutton, 1982). Although the examples in his study are limited to windows in New York City, Sturm's survey of style, technique, cultural context, patronage, and European influences applies to all American stained glass. The photographs by James Chotas are a compendium of American stained glass styles. Sturm's annotated bibliography is the most thorough guide to the subject available. An influential book on Neo-Gothic styles in stained glass, and still a valuable source for the taste of its times, is Charles J. Connick's *Adventures in Color and Light* (New York: Random House, 1937).

The Keck Studio Archives in the Onondaga Historical Association, Syracuse, New York, contains a very extensive collection of business papers, photographs, watercolor sketches, cartoons, tools, and other memorabilia covering the entire period of the Studio's existence. It also contains many hours of untranscribed tape-recorded interviews with Stanley Worden made between 1978 and 1980, and unedited videotape footage of interviews with Worden made in the summer of 1982. The Keck Studio Archives is as yet uncatalogued. Other historical papers, artwork, and glass from the Keck Studio exist in private collections.

Concerning the Keck Studio, see Cleota Reed Gabriel's *The Arts and Crafts Ideal: The Ward House—An Architect and His Craftsmen* (Syracuse: IDEA, Inc., 1978); Dorothy Frances Terino's M.A. thesis, "A History of the Henry Keck Stained Glass Studio" (Syracuse University, 1982); and Syracuse newspaper clippings preserved in the Keck Archives.

For the upstate New York Arts and Crafts Movement background for the Keck Studio, see Coy L. Ludwig's *The Arts and Crafts Movement in New York State (1980s–1920s)* (Hamilton, N.Y.: Gallery Association of New York State, 1983); Mary Ann Smith's *Gustav Stickley, the Craftsman* (Syracuse: Syracuse University Press, 1983); and Peg Weiss' *Adelaide Alsop Robineau: Glory in Porcelain* (Syracuse: Syracuse University Press, 1981). The broader scope of the Arts and

Crafts Movement is the subject of Robert Judson Clark's *The Arts and Crafts Movement in America 1876–1916,* exhibition catalogue (Princeton: Princeton University Press, 1972); Gillian Naylor's *The Arts and Crafts Movement: A Study of its Sources, Ideals and Influence on Design Theory* (Cambridge, Ma.: MIT Press, 1971); and Nikolaus Pevsner's *Pioneers of Modern Design* (London, 1936; Penguin Books, 1960).

Select List of Keck Studio Windows

HIS LIST includes most of the significant installations of Keck Studio windows. It is organized alphabetically by state, city, or town. In the case of New York State locations, the county is noted parenthetically. Many buildings listed contain stained glass by makers other than the Keck Studio. The inclusive dates of the Studio's work, the subjects of major figure windows, and their location in the buildings are given when known. The names of window artists are noted by initials in parentheses as follows: When two names are noted, the first is the chief designer and the second, following the hyphen, the principal painter of the window. This citation is not the whole story, for as Stanley Worden notes, "while at times some windows were painted *entirely by one person, this would be on rare occasions.* Usually everyone in the art department did some painting on each window. Even men from the shop like Bill Yost would help out with stenciling or other operations considered glass painting when we were hard pressed in our department and work was slack in the shop area. Artists we had like Quentin Blay helped out on jobs by other artists, such as Ronald Shaw's important Fort Bragg 82nd Airborne window. Even in the designing of a window, many times it was two or three of us who had a hand in it before the sketch was completed. It is next to impossible to recall the artist who painted what, except in rare instances— except for the years I was doing most of the designing, cartooning, and painting. Mentioning cartooning, this is just as important an operation in the making of a window as the designing and even more important to have an artist who can draw cartoons."

(A) ERNEST ASHCROFT (1963–1968)
(GB) GUSTAV BERNHARDT (1925–1927)

Figure 33. Artist Stanley Worden painting *Knight*.

   (B) QUENTIN BLAY (late 1950s–1961)
   (JB) JOSEPH BURION (1929–1931)
   (H) ROBERT HEIM (1946–1958)
   (K) HENRY KECK (1913–1954)
  (Ke) MARION KELSO (DANN) (off and on)
   (L) NORMAN LINDNER (1913–1920s, free-lance artist)
   (P) THOMAS PORTER (1924–1929)
   (R) ADOLPH ROTENECKER (1940s–1950s, free-lance artist)
   (S) RONALD SHAW (1955–1962)
  (W) STANLEY WORDEN (1922–1974)
   (Y) CHARLES YOUNG (1913–1933, free-lance artist)

It has not been possible to ascertain the condition of most of the installations, but when a window is known to have been removed or destroyed, this fact is noted. The names of the buildings have been taken from the Keck Studio order books and other contemporary records. The Keck Studio made more than 20,000 orders, including restorations, very simple windows, installations of protection glass, repairs, and residential work. Records for most of these jobs were not kept and so have been excluded from the list.

Cleota Reed, Dorothy Terino, and Stanley Worden compiled the list between 1977 and 1984, funded in part by a grant from the New York State Council on the Arts.

ALABAMA
    Jasper
        Goodsprings Baptist Church, 1945
        Christ in Garden (W)

ARKANSAS
    Hot Springs
        synagogue, before 1930
        Ten Commandments (W)

COLORADO
Denver

Park Hill Methodist Church, 1956
four *Evangelists* circular window, four nave windows with
emblems (K-S)

CONNECTICUT
Hartford

synagogue, *circa* 1926 (Temple Beth Israel?)
eighteen emblem windows (K, P, W) building demolished,
fate of windows unknown

Naugatuck

St. Paul's Evangelical Lutheran Church, 1965
twelve emblem windows (A)

New London

First Baptist Church, 1936
three-panel figure window and seven small windows

North Grosvenordale

Emanuel Lutheran Church, 1969
two emblem windows with Gothic top

Wapping

St. Peter's Episcopal Church, 1965
six St. Peter nave windows (A)

Waterbury

Beth El Synagogue, 1930
all windows

DELAWARE
Claymont

Archmere, John Jacob Raskob residence, 1917
Grape Arbor, forty-eight-foot-square opalescent skylight (K)
now Archmere Academy

Wilmington
> Mt. Salem Methodist Church, 1943
> sixteen ornamental windows with emblems (W)

Wyoming
> Wyoming Methodist Church, 1956
> four double-hung windows (W)

DISTRICT OF COLUMBIA
> Church of the Nativity, 1926
> *Nativity, Ascension, Angel* (P)

FLORIDA
Clearwater
> Episcopal Church of the Ascension, 1940
> *Ascension* (W)

Daytona Beach
> Traveler's Community Church, mid-1920s
> *Nativity* (L-P)

Fort Pierce
> St. Andrew's Episcopal Church, 1935
> *Christ Knocking* (K), *Christ Blessing Children* (W), *Christ in Field of Lilies* (W)

Jacksonville
> Congregation Ahworth Chesid, 1956
> four balcony windows with symbols (W)

Madison
> Baptist Church, 1939
> *Baptism* (W)

FLORIDA (*cont.*)

Melbourne Beach

Community Chapel, 1958
opalescent window with emblems (W-S)

Miami

St. Sophia Hellenic Orthodox Community Church, 1949–1951
Crucifixion and circular windows, angels' heads (W)

Miami Beach

St. John on the Lake First Methodist Church, 1957, 1958
seven ornamentals (W)

Tampa

Redemptorist Fathers' Home, 1940
three windows (W)

GEORGIA

Albany

Albany Hebrew Congregation, 1949
transom with symbol (W)

Temple B'nai Israel, 1949
twelve windows (W)

Augusta

Walton Way Temple, Congregation Children of Israel, 1955–1964
nave, transom, rabbi's study, all windows (W)

Savannah

St. Mary's Home, 1937
Christ Blessing Children, Holy Family (W)

South Lumber City

Methodist Episcopal Church, 1939 (W)

IDAHO
>   Blackfoot
>   >   St. Paul's Episcopal Church, 1947
>   >   circular ornamental window (W)

ILLINOIS
>   Chicago
>   >   St. Bartholomew's Episcopal Church, 1922-1923
>   >   crucifixion window (L-K)

>   Danville
>   >   Lakeview Memorial Hospital, 1960
>   >   *Good Shepherd* (S)

>   DeKalb
>   >   First Methodist Church, 1948
>   >   small intricate windows with symbols (W)
>   >   windows sold

>   La Rose
>   >   Crow Meadow Presbyterian Church, 1962
>   >   crucifix-shaped window (W)

>   Woodson
>   >   Woodson Christian Church, 1951
>   >   transom and side lights (W)

INDIANA
>   Ambia
>   >   The Christian Church, 1945
>   >   ten windows, stock design #2

>   Greencastle
>   >   Gobin Memorial Methodist Episcopal Church of DePauw
>   >   University, 1937–1969
>   >   all windows, large job, pictorials (W)

INDIANA (*cont.*)
Indianapolis
St. John's Roman Catholic Church, 1942
all windows, large job, ornamental painted (W)

IOWA
Carroll
St. Lawrence Roman Catholic Church, 1952
twelve figure windows (W)

KANSAS
Beloit
Presbyterian Church, 1950–1953
diamond lights with cross, six windows, stock designs

Leavenworth
St. Mary's Roman Catholic Academy, before 1922
Mater del Rosa, St. Paul circle (Y), *St. Catherine* circle,
Isaiah (K), *St. Agnes, Boy Christ* (K), *St. Cecilia, St. Francis
Xavier, St. Vincent* circular (Y, K), *Virgin Mary*

McPherson
First Christian Church, 1947
Christ in the Temple (W)

KENTUCKY
Louisville
Crescent Hill Baptist Church, 1959
Christ, Light of the World (S)

MAINE
Presque Isle
Bethany Baptist Church, 1966, 1970
Good Shepherd, four windows with symbols (W-A)

Sherman Mills
    Washburn Memorial Church, 1966
    angel with organ (A)

MARYLAND
    Baltimore
        Govanstown Presbyterian Church, 1943
        Ruth (K)

    Bethesda
        Bethesda First Baptist Church, 1942
        rose window with symbols (W)

    Brownsville
        St. Luke's Eiscopal Church, 1949
        Good Shepherd (W)

    Dundalk
        St. George's Episcopal Church, late 1930s–1970
        St. George in rectory (gone); narthex, *Isaiah's Prophecy;*
        altar, *Resurrection;* baptistry, four nave windows (W, S)

    Ellicot City
        St. John's Episcopal Church, 1943
        Blessed Virgin (W)

    Glen Burnie
        St. Alban's Episcopal Church, 1945, 1965
        Christ Blessing, Nativity (K), *Good Samaritan* (A)

    North Baltimore
        Protestant Church, 1942
        Boy Christ with Book circular window (K)

    Smithburg
        St. Ann's Episcopal Church, 1963
        St. Cecilia, King David (S-W)

MASSACHUSETTS
  Brockton
    St. Joseph's Manor Nursing Home Roman Catholic Chapel, 1967
    fifteen windows, two figures, and passion symbols (A)

  Leominster
    Leominster Methodist Church, 1968
    Descending Dove (W)

  Lowell
    United Methodist Church, pre-1930, 1972
    circular window

MICHIGAN
  Battle Creek
    First Methodist Church, 1963–1965
    Blessing Children, Good Shepherd, Gethsemane (W)

  Flint
    Court Street Methodist Church, 1961–1965
    chapel, eight *Beatitudes* (W-S); balcony, *Christ in Garden, Prodigal Son, Good Samaritan, Resurrection*; nave (A); *Twelve Apostles* (A); altar, *Come Unto Me* (W)

  Jasper
    Methodist Church, pre-1930

  Lapeer
    Trinity United Methodist Church, 1970
    five nave windows with symbols, end windows (W, A)

  Pelkie
    Finnish Evangelical Lutheran Church, 1948
    opalescent window

St. Ignace
>
> Zion Lutheran Church, 1940s
> two adoring angels (W)

MISSISSIPPI
Brandon
>
> Brandon Methodist Church, 1958
> circular *Light of the World*, six nave and vestibule windows
> (W-S)

Jackson
>
> Trinity Evangelical Lutheran Church, 1949
> two 3-D windows (W-K), revolving world globe outside
> window (K-W), twelve windows in all

Macon
>
> Mission Church of Corpus Christi, 1953–1960
> two ornamental windows (W)

NEBRASKA
Bridgeport
>
> First Presbyterian Church, 1967
> sixteen emblems (A)

Gordon
>
> St. Mark's Episcopal Church, 1957
> *Christ the King* (W)

NEW HAMPSHIRE
Derry
>
> Church of the Transfiguration (Protestant), 1964
> three pictorial windows (W)

NEW HAMPSHIRE (*cont.*)
    Spofford
        Spofford Methodist Church, 1961
        Christ in Garden (S)

NEW JERSEY
    Califon
        Califon Methodist Church, 1962
        all windows, ornamental with symbols (W)

    Morristown
        Smith Memorial Chapel, Morristown Hospital, 1952
        Christ the Healer with portraits (W)

    Newark
        First Methodist Church, 1916
        (K)

    Perth Amboy
        unknown church, before 1922, Episcopal Church
        Resurrection (K)

    Rahway
        St. Paul's Episcopal Church, 1961–1967
        large two-panel nave window, *Life of St. John* (W-S), door
        lights, small circle (W)

    South Amboy
        Christ Episcopal Church, 1920s and 1930s, 1952–1956
        Ascension 1930s (W); *Supper at Emmaus, Washing Christ's
        Feet* (W)

    South Orange
        First Presbyterian and Trinity Church, 1945–1951
        St. Michael and Twelve Virtues rose window; sixteen figure
        windows in nave; vestibule; two rose windows; Old and
        New Testaments in transept (W)

Trenton
> Evangelical Lutheran Church of St. Bartholomew, 1938
> ornamental (W)

NEW MEXICO
Carlsbad
> First Presbyterian Church, 1952–1954
> *Nativity, Blessing Children, Crucifixion* three-panel; altar
> window; seven emblem windows (W)
>
> Grace Episcopal Church, 1945–1955
> *Christ Victorious, Mother and Child, Baptism of Christ,*
> *Crucifixion, Nativity, Christ Blessing Children* (W)

NEW YORK
Adams Center (Jefferson County)
> Seventh Day Baptist Church, 1927, 1939
> *Good Shepherds* (P), *Easter Morn* (W)

Albany (Albany County)
> Bethany Reformed Community Church, 1966
> *Christ in Gethsemane* (W)
>
> Roman Catholic Convent, before 1930
> 538 Morris Street
> *Fra Angelico* (W, R)
>
> Madison Avenue Presbyterian Church, 1942–1964
> all windows in church: *Good Shepherd, Baptism of Christ,*
> *Sermon on Mount, Christ Blessing Children, Purity,*
> *Humility, Christ in Garden, Woman at Well, Christ: Light*
> *of World, Boy Christ in Temple, Rich Young Ruler, The*
> *Sower, Healing Blind,* seven apse symbol windows (W).

NEW YORK—Albany (*cont.*)
> New York State Capitol Assembly Chamber hall, 1950
> *Seal of State of New York, DeWitt Clinton* and *Peter Minuit* portrait windows (David Lithgow-K)
>
> St. Anthony's Roman Catholic Church, before 1930
> all windows in church (P)
>
> Westminster Presbyterian Church, 1940, 1951
> blue diamond lights

Alexandria Bay (Jefferson County)
> Reformed Church of the Thousand Islands, 1941, 1960
> *Easter Morn* (K), *Madonna and Child* (W)
>
> St. Cyril's Roman Catholic Church, 1973
> four pair chapel windows with emblems (W)

Altamont (Albany County)
> Roman Catholic Church, circa 1925
> *St. Lucy, Resurrection, Annunciation* (P)

Altmar (Oswego County)
> St. John's Episcopal Church, 1962, 1965, gone

Altona (Clinton County)
> Trinity Church of the Nazarene, 1935
> *The Blessing Christ* (W)

Amboy Center (Oswego County)
> Methodist Church, 1950
> all windows, opalescent, ornamental with emblems

Amsterdam (Montgomery County)
> St. Joseph's Roman Catholic Convent, 1956
> seven chapel windows with emblems (W)
>
> St. Luke's Evangelical Lutheran Church, 1937
> diamond-patterned windows

St. Mary's Roman Catholic Church, 1941–1948
two circular windows after Raphael (K-R); *Christ in Gethsemane, Christ Triumphant* (W); *Immaculate Conception* altar window; *Liberty, Supper at Emmaus, St. Isaac Jogues, Kateri Tekakwitha* transept windows; *Christ and Nicodemus, Madonna and Child, Baptism of Christ* baptistry windows (W)

St. Mary's Roman Catholic Hospital, before 1930, torn down, window location unknown

St. Michael's Roman Catholic Church, 1931
Annunciation, St. John Baptist, St. Peter, Dove, all windows (B)

Apulia Station (Onondaga County)
Apulia Station Methodist Church, 1943
two opalescent windows

Auburn (Cayuga County)
First Presbyterian Church, 1962–1972, 1975
twelve nave windows (A), church torn down, some windows rebuilt to fit new church

Lake Avenue Christian Church, 1968
cross and book, torn down

St. John's Episcopal Church, 1960
three emblems (S, W)

St. Luke's Lutheran Church, 1949, 1961–1962
rose *Gethsemane* (K), nave (W), door lights (W)

Second Presbyterian Church, 1963

Trinity United Methodist Church, 1971
three symbols (W)

Westminster Presbyterian church, 1932
opalescent (?)

NEW YORK (*cont.*)

Augusta (Madison County)
Augusta Presbyterian Church, 1947
all opalescent in the church, with symbols (W)

Bainbridge (Chenango County)
St. Peter's Episcopal Church, 1926, 1964
Faith and Love, two-panel figure window (P), one two-panel window with symbols (A)

Baldwinsville (Onondaga County)
Grace Episcopal Church, circa 1925, 1958
burned down, two original windows in vestibule of new church

St. Mary's Roman Catholic Church Convent, 1956
five ornamental windows

Batavia (Genesee County)
St. Paul's Evangelical Lutheran Church, 1951–1968
Bethany door lights (A), sixteen figure windows (W), *Come Unto Me, Martin Luther, St. Paul, Rose, Christ Blessing Children, Good Shepherd, Ascension, Ecce Homo, Gethsemane, Nativity, Christ in Temple, Light of World, Resurrection, I Am Vine, Christ the King* (W)

Belfort (Lewis County)
St. Vincent de Paul Catholic Mission Church, 1963–1964
six two-lancet windows

Belle Isle (Onondaga County)
Belle Isle Methodist Church, 1944, 1964, 1968
all windows, door lights, emblems, transom (W)

Binghamton (Broome County)
Central Baptist Church, 1968–1969
one large window with cross (W)

Christ Episcopal Church, 1954
two memorial windows in vestibule (W)

John Hus Presbyterian Church, 1966–1967
transom, six symbol windows (A)

St. Ann's Convent, 1949
four windows with emblems

St. Ann's Roman Catholic Church, 1965
six sacrament windows, large three-panel *Good Shepherd*
(W-A)

St. Catherine's Parish Catholic Church, 1964
Priesthood in rectory (W), front door window

St. Michael's Catholic Church, 1930

St. Thomas Aquinas Catholic Church, 1953
three figures: *Sacred Heart, Jesus, Mary and Joseph* (W);
one circular: *Franciscan Arms* (W), fate unknown

Trinity Episcopal Church, 1939
Boy Christ in Temple, Joseph, Christ the Carpenter (W)

St. Vincent de Paul
windows (W)

West End Presbyterian Church, 1932
Christ, Come unto Me (W)

Bolivar (Allegheny County)
Protestant Church, 1922
Angel at Tomb (K)

Bowens Corners (Oswego County)
Methodist Church, 1934

Bridgeport (Madison County)
Bridgeport Methodist Church, 1944, 1958
Christ Knocking (W),
burned and replaced (W-S)

NEW YORK (*cont.*)
    Brooklyn (Kings County)
        All Saints Episcopal Church, 1944–1945
        Christ and Faithful Servant (K)

    Brownville (Jefferson County)
        St. Paul's Episcopal Church, 1959
        inscriptions

    Buffalo (Erie County)
        North Park Lutheran Church, 1964–1968
        all stained glass in the church,
        Ascension: three panel *Trinity; Good Shepherd:* 12 figure
        groups (W-A)

        Salem Evangelical Lutheran Church, 1950–1966
        all windows in the church

    Burnt Hills (Saratoga County)
        Church with *St. Peter* window, circa 1924–1928 (P)

    Camden (Oneida)
        Catholic Church, circa 1924
        Crucifixion (P)

    Camillus (Onondaga County)
        Camillus Baptist Church, 1916, 1963, 1969
        ornamental, restored after church fire

        St. Joseph's Roman Catholic Church, 1952–1953, 1966
        ornamental (W).
        new church built, stations of the cross windows only;
        church closed, turned into apartment house, old windows
        gone.

        St. Michael's Lutheran Church, 1963–1970
        Presentation, Crucifixion, Betrayal, Temptation, Nativity
        (A), and others

Canastota (Oneida County)
        Canastota High School, 1926–1974 (K-W)
        Spirit of Freedom, etc., one for each year (W)

        Canastota Presbyterian Church, 1940, 1962
        Good Shepherd (W), other large windows

Canton (St. Lawrence County)
        First Baptist Church, 1954, 1973
        four windows: *Head of Christ*, etc., *Mighty Fortress, Faith,*
        Hope and Charity, In This Sign Conquer, Dove and Book
        opal (W)

Cape Vincent (Jefferson County)
        St. John's Episcopal Church, before 1930
        Field of Lilies (K), opalescent windows

Cazenovia (Madison County)
        St. James Roman Catholic Church, circa 1930s
        church torn down, one window moved to new church,
        crucifixion center panel

Cedarvale (Onondaga County)
        Cedarvale Methodist Church, 1960
        two vestibule windows, *Open Book, Alpha and Omega* (W)

Central Square (Oswego County)
        St. Michael's Roman Catholic Church, 1952–1953
        opalescent ornamental

Champlain (Clinton County)
        church, n. d.
        Good Shepherd, St. John, Angel, transom

Cicero (Onondaga County)
        Cicero Community Methodist Church, 1963
        circular *Gethsemane* (W)

NEW YORK (*cont.*)

Cincinnatus (Cortland County)
First Baptist Church, 1958
ornamentals (W)

First Methodist Church, 1961–1964
six figure windows, *Good Shepherd, Christ Knocking,
Christ Blessing, King David, Come Unto Me, Boy Christ in
Temple* (S), *Evangelists* (W), *Trinity* (A)

Clayton (Jefferson County)
Christ Episcopal Church, early 1920s
Annunciation (K), opalescent figure window

Cobleskill (Schoharie County)
Catholic Church, circa 1925–1927
Boy Christ in Temple (GB-P), *Christ Blessing*, circular
Lamb of God (P)

Methodist Church, 1946
Good Shepherd (W)

Cohoes (Albany County)
St. Cecilia Catholic Church, 1920s
St. Peter, St. Valentine, Madonna of Rosary (G-B), *St.
Cecilia* (P), and others

Cold Spring on the Hudson (Putnam County)
Timme Family Mausoleum, 1940s
Crossing the Bar (W), Christ figure with palm

Corning (Steuben County)
St. Patrick's Roman Catholic Church, 1931

Cortland (Cortland County)
First Methodist Church, 1954
four door lights, four *Evangelists* windows (W)

First Presbyterian Church, 1966
diamond lights

Memorial Baptist Church, 1946
Come Unto Me, Good Shepherd (W)

St. Anthony of Padua, 1920s
old church gone
St. Anthony of Padua, St. Rocco (Y-K)

St. Anthony's Roman Catholic Church, 1953–1954
eighteen figure windows, all windows *St. Anthony* circular:
*Assumption, St. Lucy, St. Damion, St. Cosmos, St. Francis,
St. Joseph, Sacred Heart of Jesus, St. Ann, Our Lady of
Perpetual Help, St. Peter, Immaculate Conception,
Ascension, Coronation of Blessed Virgin, St. Anthony, Our
Lady of Mt. Carmel, St. Michael, St. Anthony and Child*

St. Mary's Roman Catholic Church, circa 1923
nine ornamentals (K-W)
first windows Worden painted for Keck Studio

Dannemora (Clinton County)
St. Joseph's Roman Catholic Church, 1931, 1942
transepts: *Crucifixion, Nativity, Annunciation, Christ in
Workshop* (W)

Delhi (Delaware County)
First Baptist Church, 1960
ornamentals

Delmar (Albany County)
Delmar Reformed Church, 1966
eleven emblems, one inscription (A)

Deposit (Broome-Delaware Counties)
Catholic Church, 1920s
St. Peter, St. Paul (P), and other windows

DeWitt (Onondaga County)
First Universalist Church, 1961
large rose window (S)

Holy Cross Roman Catholic Mission, 1949–1950
symbols (W)

Holy Cross Rectory, 1950–1951

NEW YORK (*cont.*)
Dolgeville (Herkimer-Fulton Counties)
St. Joseph's Roman Catholic Church, 1931
memorial

Durhamville (Oneida County)
St. Francis Roman Catholic Church, 1971
very simple cross in circular (W)

St. Mary's Irish Ridge Roman Catholic Church, 1950
six ornamentals

Earlville (Chenango-Madison Counties)
Grace Episcopal Church, before 1930

East Syracuse (Onondaga County)
Emmanuel Episcopal Church, 1957
opalescent emblems (W)

East Syracuse School, before 1930
kindergarten windows

East Williamson (Wayne County)
Dutch Reformed Church, 1944, 1962–1963
Christ Blessing Children circle window (K); one ornamental
window

Edmeston (Otsego County)
Second Baptist Church, 1948

Edwards (St. Lawrence County)
Assembly of God Church, 1955
cross windows, *Come Unto Me* (W)

Elbridge (Onondaga County)
Community Church, 1936
opalescent window

Elizabethtown (Essex County)
  St. Elizabeth's Roman Catholic Church, 1932–1936
  twelve figure windows: *Sacred Heart of Mary, Sacred Heart of Joseph, St. Ann, Our Lady of Perpetual Help, St. Peter, Immaculate Conception, Ascension, Coronation of The Blessed Virgin, St. Anthony, Our Lady of Mt. Carmel, St. Michael, St. Anthony and Child* (W)

Elizaville (Columbia County)
  St. Thomas Evangelical Lutheran Church, 1960
  plain windows

Ellisburg (Jefferson County)
  Methodist Church, 1955
  small ornamental, *Christ in Garden* circular (W)

Elmira (Chemung County)
  Centenary Methodist Church, 1932
  seventy windows and doors

Endicott (Broome County)
  First Presbyterian Church, 1953–1954
  eleven narthex, simple grape and wheat design (W)

  St. Paul's Episcopal Church, 1956, 1968
  three-panel chancel: *Christ the King, Crucifixion, Resurrection* (W-S), *Madonna and Child* (A)

Fabius (Onondaga County)
  Methodist Church, 1946–1947, 1955
  eight opalescent, circular with emblems, plain opalescent

Fairmount (Onondaga County)
  Holy Family Roman Catholic Church Convent, 1950
  deep blue ornamentals (W)

Fayetteville (Onondaga County)
  Trinity Episcopal Church, 1971
  Holy Trinity circular (W)

NEW YORK (*cont.*)

    Findley Lake (Chautauqua County)
        United Brethren Church, 1943
        opalescent emblems

    Fonda (Montgomery County)
        St. Cecilia's Roman Catholic Church and Rectory, circa 1925
        all windows: *Sacred Heart* (K), *K. Tekakwitha, Isaac Jogues, Our Lady of Lourdes, Christ in Gethsemane, Annunciation, Baptism of Christ, Boy Christ in Temple, Road to Emmaus* (P)

    Fort Plain (Montgomery County)
        St. Paul's Lutheran Church, 1936
        Christ in Gethsemane circular (W)

    Friendship (Allegheny County)
        First Baptist Church, 1938
        Good Shepherd (W)

    Fulton (Oswego County)
        First Baptist Church, 1915
        (K)

        Holy Family Roman Catholic Church, 1953
        ornamental, emblems (W)

        Immaculate Conception Roman Catholic Church, 1935, 1948, 1963
        all windows, baptistry *Seven Sacraments* (W), *Immaculate Conception*, 1963 (W)

        Fred N. Palmer Mausoleum, 1947
        two opalescent windows (W)

        State Street Methodist Church, 1965–1973
        all windows, symbols (W-A), *Christ Knocking* (W)

    Gasport (Niagara County)
        Zion Lutheran Church, 1968–1969
        all windows, sixteen symbols (W-A)

Germantown (Columbia County)
Roman Catholic Church of the Resurrection, 1933–1934
eighteen figure windows, including: *Kateri Tekakwitha, St. Cecilia, Prodigal Son, St. Anne, St. Theresa, St. Agnes, St. Rose of Lima, St. Anthony, St. Stanislas, St. Costka, St. Joan*

Gloversville (Fulton County)
Fremont Street Methodist Church, 1950–1951
Good Shepherd (W)

Our Lady of Mount Carmel Roman Catholic Church, 1924–1929
sixteen nave figure windows, series: *Life of Christ* (P)

Sacred Heart Roman Catholic Church, 1938
all windows, including three circular windows: *St. Agnes and Guardian Angel, Visitation and Annunciation, Archangel*; World War I memorial (W)

St. Mary's Roman Catholic Church, before 1930
opalescent circular transept windows, *Mary and Child* and *John, Christ Crowning Mary* (after Raphael) (GB-K)

Young Women's Christian Association, 1949

Gouverneur (St. Lawrence County)
Gouverneur High School, before 1930
classical subject figure window (K)

Granville (Washington County)
Methodist Church, 1952
rose window (W)

Hamden (Delaware County)
Calvary Baptist Church, before 1930
Good Shepherd (Y-K)

Hamilton (Madison County)
St. Mary's Roman Catholic Church, mid-1920s
figure windows, including: *Immaculate Conception, St.*

NEW YORK—Hamilton (*cont.*)
 Matthew, St. Mark, St. Luke, St. John, St. Anthony of Padua with Christ Child, prophets (P)

Hannibal (Oswego County)
 Raymond Cooper Mausoleum, 1945

 Our Lady of the Rosary Roman Catholic Church, 1958–1959
 circle window, *Our Lady of the Rosary* (W-S)

Hastings (Oswego County)
 Hastings Presbyterian Church, 1959–1960
 ornamental opalescent symbols, *Ten Commandments* emblem

Hollis (Queens County)
 Evangelical Lutheran Church of the Holy Trinity, 1940
 Christ Blessing Children, Boy Christ in Temple (W-Reiger)

Homer (Cortland County)
 Homer Congregational Church, 1956
 two simple windows

Hoosick Falls (Rensselaer County)
 First Baptist Church, 1946
 two ornamental windows

Hudson (Columbia County)
 Emmanuel Lutheran Church, before 1930
 Baptism of Christ (P)

 First Reformed Church, 1934–1942
 destroyed by fire; windows in new church: *Sermon on Mount, Good Shepherd* (W)

Ilion (Herkimer County)
 Calvary Episcopal Church, before 1930

St. Augustine's Episcopal Church, 1948–1949
ornamental rose (W)

Ithaca (Tompkins County)
Kent Steak House Restaurant, 1964
(W)

St. Catherine's Greek Orthodox Church, 1965–1967
Resurrection (A), two circular windows: *Dove, Silver Chalice* (W-A)

State Street Methodist Church, 1934
opalescent windows

Jamesville (Onondaga County)
St. Mary's Roman Catholic Church, 1935, 1962
St. Cecilia, St. Anthony of Padua, St. Joseph and Child, St. Vincent, St. John as Child, Christ Child, Sacred Heart of Jesus, Sacred Heart of Mary (W), vestibule, symbols, *Infant of Prague* (W)

Johnson City (Broome County)
Blessed Sacrament Roman Catholic Church Convent Chapel, 1958–1959
St. Joseph the Workman (W), all windows

Winslow Hospital Chapel, 1966
fountain *Peace* (A)

St. James Roman Catholic Church, circa 1935
St. Vincent de Paul, Nativity, Resurrection, altar window, symbols of *Blessed Sacrament* (W)

Johnstown (Fulton County)
First Presbyterian Church, 1952–1953

Johnstown Reformed Church, 1942–1944
Gethsemane circular (W)

St. Patrick's Roman Catholic Church, 1922
all windows (L-K)

NEW YORK—Johnstown (*cont.*)
St. Paul's Lutheran Church, 1936–1942
Rich Young Man, Gethsemane, St. Paul, Christ Knocking (W)
no longer a church, fate of windows unknown

Jordan (Onondaga County)
St. Patrick's Roman Catholic Church, 1957–1963
big job, *Christ the King* nave window (W, S), sacristy,
Easter Morn balcony (W-S), door lights

Kellogsville (Cayuga County)
Methodist Church, 1955–1957
circular *Gethsemane* (W), all opalescent windows

Kirkville (Onondaga County)
Christ Community Church, before 1930; became United
Church of Christ, 1972–1973
Christ Blessing Children (W), two side ornamentals with
symbols

Kirkwood (Broome County)
Kirkwood School, 1957
six windows with animal subjects for kindergarten designed
by architect Walter Paul Bowen, Binghamton

Lafayette (Onondaga County)
St. Joseph's Roman Catholic Church, 1961–1962
door lights and transom

Lairdsville (Madison County)
Lairdsville Methodist Church, 1946
all windows in church

Lakeland (Onondaga County)
Our Lady of Peace Roman Catholic Church, before 1930
destroyed by fire

Lake Placid (Essex County)
St. Eustace Episcopal Church, 1963–1966
Good Shepherd (A), *Standing Triumphant* and *Holy Trinity*
circles (W-A)

Larchmont (Westchester County)
        Episcopal Church, 1944?
        one window, *Christ and the Faithful Servant* (W)

Liberty (Sullivan County)
        Episcopal Church of the Holy Communion, 1930s, 1941–
        1942, 1951–1955
        Annunciation, Coronation, St. Anne, Teaching Mary,
        Purification (W), *Boy Christ in Temple, Crucifixion* (K),
        church gone, windows removed to another Episcopal
        church on Hudson River

        St. Paul's Evangelical Lutheran Church, 1947–1950
        opalescent windows, some of Keck's last work

Lisbon (St. Lawrence County)
        United Presbyterian Church, 1966
        Come Unto Me (W-A)

Little Genesee (Allegheny County)
        Seventh Day Adventist Church, 1935
        ten windows

Liverpool (Onondaga County)
        First United Presbyterian Church, 1970–1971
        repair only

        Maurer Funeral Home, 1966–1967
        ornamental transom (W)

        St. Matthew's Episcopal Church, 1951–1952
        Christ the King (W), church burned, windows saved and
        removed to new church

        St. Paul's Lutheran Church, circa 1914, 1964–1965
        Christ Blessing Children (K) removed to new church, four
        Evangelist windows (A)

Lockport (Niagara County)
        St. Joseph's Roman Catholic Church, 1955–1956
        Beatitudes rose window, nave *Christ in the Workshop,*

NEW YORK—Lockport (*cont.*)

thirteen small figures of saints, series of sixteen, life of Joseph and Christ: *Death of Joseph, Joseph's Return to Nazareth, Holy Family, Nazareth, Circumcision of Divine Child, Flight into Egypt, Abraham and Melchisedeck, Last Supper, Finding Jesus in Temple, Espousal of Joseph and Mary, No Room in the Inn, St. Joseph Patron Universal Church, Joseph and Jesus in Workshop, Nativity, Joseph Present at Adoration of Shepherds, St. Joseph our Patron, St. Joseph at Adoration of Wise Men* (W-S)

St. Peter's Lutheran Church, 1954–1955
Come Unto Me (K)
church burned down?

Lowell (Oneida County)
Lowell United Methodist Church, 1972
circular (W)

Lyons (Wayne County)
Grace Episcopal Church, 1955
three-panel nave window *"I Have Overcome the World"* (W)

McConnellsville (Oneida County)
McConnellsville Community Church, 1952
Christ in Garden of Gethsemane circular (W)

Madrid (St. Lawrence County)
Church (Reverend Creedon), before 1930
St. John the Baptist as a Boy (L-K)

Malone (Franklin County)
Temple Beth El, 1950
one window (W)

Manlius (Onondaga County)
St. Anne's Roman Catholic Church, circa 1916
St. Anne (K), church torn down, windows sold, no stained glass in new church

Marcellus (Onondaga County)
>First Presbyterian Church, before 1930

>Marcellus Episcopal Church, 1922
>altar windows, *St. James, St. Andrew, St. John, St. Peter,*
>etc. (K)

>St. Francis Xavier Roman Catholic Church, 1945–1947,
>1961
>*Annunciation, Flight into Egypt, Nativity, Boy Christ in
>Temple, Baptism, Marriage at Cana, Good Shepherd,
>Charging Apostles, Triumphal Entry, Last Supper, Agony in
>Garden* (W)

Marietta (Onondaga County)
>Marietta United Christian Church, 1959, 1971
>emblems (W)

Mattydale (Onondaga County)
>Calvary Evangelical Church, 1934
>fifteen ornamentals

>Calvary United Methodist Episcopal Church, 1935

Mexico (Oswego County)
>Methodist Church, before 1930

>St. Mary's Roman Catholic Church, 1915, 1944–1957
>*St. Cecilia* (K), *Fra Angelico* angels, *St. Pius X, St. Patrick,
>St. Anne and Blessed Mother, St. James, St. Isaac Jogues,
>Kateri Tekakwitha* (W)

Middletown (Orange County)
>St. Joseph's Roman Catholic Church, 1932–1941
>all windows: nave, *Seven Sacraments, World War I
>Memorial,* balcony, *Christ the King,* sacristy, circular
>clerestory windows, narthex (W)

Minoa (Onondaga County)
>Minoa Methodist Church, 1957–1964
>all windows, modern design, symbols (W)

NEW YORK—Minoa (*cont.*)
>
> St. Mary's Roman Catholic Church, 1936, 1940
> *St. Louis, St. Anthony with Child, St. Elizabeth, St. Francis* (W), all windows

Monticello (Sullivan County)
>
> St. John's Episcopal Church, 1959–1971
> *Adoration of Magi* (W-S)

Montour Falls (Schuyler County)
>
> First Baptist Church, 1948–1959
> opalescent ornamentals

Moravia (Cayuga County)
>
> Casowasco Central New York Conference of Methodist Churches, 1952

Munnsville (Madison County)
>
> First Congregational Church, 1972
> opalescent circular window (W)
>
> St. Theresa Roman Catholic Church, before 1930
> early Porter windows

New Berlin (Chenango County)
>
> St. Andrew's Episcopal Chapel, 1934, 1939
> opalescent windows (K-W), *Seven Doves of Holy Spirit* circular window (W)

New Haven (Oswego County)
>
> Methodist Church, 1964–1965
> *St. Cecilia* (A)

New York Mills (Oneida County)
>
> St. Mary's Roman Catholic Church, 1958–1960
> sacristy door windows (W-S)

Newburgh (Orange County)
>
> First Congregational Church, mid-1920s, 1940
> *Three Marys at Tomb* (P), *Crucifixion* (Y), plain windows

Italian Institute, before 1930
Angel, Christ Knocking, Good Shepherd (L), *Boy Christ in Temple* (K)

Niagara Falls (Niagara County)
Church of the Redeemer, 1954
Christ the King (W)

North Granville (Washington County)
All Saints Episcopal Church, 1967–1968
Two windows with emblems (W)

North Syracuse (Onondaga County)
First Christian Assembly Church, 1961
Two windows

Residence, Dr. Marlow, 1964

St. Rose of Lima Roman Catholic Church, 1949–1968
all windows: *St. Rose of Lima* transept; evangelists; *Sacred Heart of Jesus, Immaculate Heart of Mary*; three-panel windows: *St. Michael, St. Anne, St. Francis of Assisi, St. Theresa, and St. Anthony with Child* (W)

St. Thomas Episcopal Church, 1959, 1962
large window with symbols (W)

Norwich (Chenango County)
Residence, Mayor Zuber, before 1930
Dancing, Feasting (W)

M. C. Eaton Residence, 1933
Eight rathskeller windows
now Norwich Jewish Center

Odessa (Schuyler County)
Odessa Baptist Church, 1962–1963
Come Unto Me (W)

NEW YORK (*cont.*)

Ogdensburg (St. Lawrence County)
Chancery, Diocese of Ogdensburg, 1963–1964
bishop's crest (W)

Protestant Church and Synagogue, St. Lawrence State
Hospital, 1958
stained glass around top of walls (W)

St. Mary's Academy, 1960
one window in door

Old Forge (Herkimer County)
Niccolls Memorial Church, 1964
Head of Christ (W)

Olean (Cattaraugus County)
Showers Memorial Evangelical United Brethren Church,
1958–1959
Come Unto Me (W-S)

Oneida (Madison County)
First Presbyterian Church, 1935
I Am the Way (K-W)

First Methodist Church, circa 1925
all windows, nave and *Angel and Chalice* (GB), balcony and
Ascension (P)

St. John's Episcopal Church, 1945–1946
St. John the Divine, Good Shepherd (W)

St. Joseph's Roman Catholic Church, 1929, 1964
*Ascension, Christ and Nicodemus, Sacred Heart,
Sacrifice of Isaac, Angel, Baptism of Christ,
Abraham and Melchisedeck* (P), *St. Cecilia* (W)

Oneida Castle (Oneida County)
St. Joseph's Community Church, 1938
Christ in Field of Lilies (W)

Oneonta (Otsego County)
Atonement Lutheran Church, 1962
Nativity, Resurrection, etc. (W)

First Presbyterian Church, 1964–1965
Gethsemane (W-A)

West End Community Baptist Church, 1958
opalescent, emblem

Oriskany (Oneida County)
Catholic Church, circa 1927
single saints (P)

Oswego (Oswego County)
Church of the Evangelists, 1925
church torn down, *Blessing Children* (P) and four other
windows gone

Congregation Adath Israel, 1968
front window *Menorah* (W)

First Methodist Episcopal Church, 1914
closed and windows gone

St. John the Evangelist Roman Catholic Church, 1969
transoms (W)

St. Paul's Roman Catholic Rectory, 1916
interior door medallions (K), church torn down

St. Paul's Roman Catholic Church, 1967–1968
large ornamental windows, some interior doors moved from
old rectory

St. Stephen's Polish Catholic Church, 1960
all windows with symbols, nave (W), *Christ, Good
Shepherd* (S)

NEW YORK (*cont.*)
        Otisco (Onondaga County)
                Otisco Presbyterian Church, 1967–1971
                Nativity, Good Shepherd, Last Supper (W-A), *Easter Morn*
                (W)

        Otter Lake (Oneida County)
                Catholic Church, pre-1920
                three-panel window (K)

        Owasco Lake (Cayuga County)
                Dutch Reformed Church, 1935
                twelve simple windows

        Oxford (Chenango County)
                Oxford Methodist Community Church, 1967–1968
                all windows, modern; nave, symbols, altar *Cross* (A-W)

                St. Joseph's Roman Catholic Church, before 1930

        Paris Hill (Oneida County)
                Catholic Church, before 1930
                (K)

        Parish (Oswego County)
                Pleasant Lawn Cemetery Association, 1964
                Head of Christ (W)

        Philadelphia (Jefferson County)
                Congregational Church, 1963
                diamond patterns

                St. Joseph's Roman Catholic Church, 1956
                emblems (W)

        Phoenix (Oswego County)
                Congregational Church, 1915
                (K)

                First Methodist Church, 1949–1950
                Behold, I Am with You Always (W)

St. Stephen's Roman Catholic Church, 1931, 1962
figure windows, *St. Francis*, *St. Dominic*, etc. (W); *Rose
window(s)*, *Baptism of Christ* (W-A)

Pittsford (Monroe County)
Christ Church, 1947–1948
Good Shepherd, *Christ Blessing*, *Nativity* (W)

Pompey (Onondaga County)
Roman Catholic Church of the Immaculate Conception,
1919, 1929–1931
St. Cecilia, *St. Theresa*, *St. Clair*, *St. Augustine*, *St. Patrick*,
St. Anne (W-W, GB)

Potsdam (St. Lawrence County)
St. Mary's Roman Catholic Convent Chapel, 1960
ten windows (W)

Pulaski (Oswego County)
Park Methodist Church, before 1930

St. John the Evangelist Roman Catholic Church, 1931
Nativity (W)

Raquette Lake (Hamilton County)
St. William's Roman Catholic Church, 1939
ornamental (W)

Ravena (Albany County)
Congregational Christian Church, 1952–1970
Crucifixion, *Christ Blessing Children*, *Jesus the Healer*, *Last
Supper*, *Boy Christ in Temple* (W-A)

Redfield (Oswego County)
St. Paul's Roman Catholic Church, 1947–1963
ornamental opalescent, symbols (W)

NEW YORK (*cont.*)
> Richland (Oswego County)
>> Methodist Church, 1931
>> all windows, diamond pattern (W)

> Rochester (Monroe County)
>> Episcopal Church of the Ascension, 1940–1949
>> *St. Michael* transept; *Raising of Lazarus, Angel, Wedding of Cana*; *Nativity* chancel (W)

> Rome (Oneida County)
>> Calvary Methodist Church, 1932
>> *Come Unto Me* (K)

>> First Presbyterian Church, 1926–1948
>> all windows

>> Griffiss Air Force Base, 1970
>> symbol windows

>> St. John's Roman Catholic Church Rectory, 1959
>> plain leaded windows

>> St. Paul's Roman Catholic Church and Rectory, 1958
>> ten door lights

>> St. Peter's Roman Catholic Convent Chapel, 1954
>> *Sacred Heart of Jesus, Immaculate Heart of Mary, Four Angelica Angels*; *Annunciation, Visitation, Nativity, Boy Christ in Temple*, nave (W), dining room, ten windows (W)

> Rosendale (Ulster County)
>> All Saints Episcopal Church, before 1930
>> *Christ Blessing Children* (P)

> Rushville (Ontario-Yates County)
>> Rushville Methodist Church, 1958
>> *I Am the Way*, circular (W)

> St. Johnsville (Montgomery County)
>> Congregational Christian Church, 1958
>> *Light of the World* after Holman Hunt (S)

Saratoga Springs (Saratoga County)
St. Patrick's Roman Catholic Church, 1931
ornamental altar window; baptistry *Baptism of Christ* (W)

Scotia (Schenectady County)
St. Andrew's Episcopal Church, 1961–1963
Baptism of Christ, *Light of the World*, *Christ Blessing Children* (S), *Good Shepherd* (W)

Scott (Cortland County)
Scott Methodist Church, 1953
ornamental (W)

Seneca Falls (Seneca County)
First Presbyterian Church, 1948
Christ Blessing Children (W)

Methodist Church, 1955
opalescent ornamental (K)

Trinity Episcopal Church, 1947
I Am the Vine (L-W), *St. Thomas* (K), *Faith* (K-W)

Sherrill (Oneida County)
St. Helena's Roman Catholic Church, 1962
symbols (W)

Sidney (Delaware County)
Methodist Church, 1933
Francis Asbury, *John Wesley* (W); church founder's window (K)

Silver Creek (Chautauqua County)
Zion Evangelical Lutheran Church, 1959
six opalescent nave windows (W)

Skaneateles (Onondaga County)
Residence, Dr. E. Basil Edson, before 1930
music room

NEW YORK—Skaneateles (*cont.*)
　　　　　St. James Episcopal Church, 1959–1961
　　　　　door lights, leaded glass symbol windows (W)

　　　　　Stella Maris Retreat House, 1954
　　　　　ornamental nave windows with emblems (W)

　　　Slingerlands (Albany County)
　　　　　Church, before 1930
　　　　　Three Marys at Tomb (P)

　　　Solvay (Onondaga County)
　　　　　St. Cecilia's Roman Catholic Church, 1962
　　　　　repairs

　　　　　St. Mary's Russian Orthodox Church, 1955
　　　　　simple diamond lights

　　　　　Solvay United Methodist Church, 1969
　　　　　Methodist emblem (W)

　　　Sonyea (Livingston County)
　　　　　Hospital for Epileptics, 1932
　　　　　Christ Healing the Sick (W)

　　　South Dayton (Cattaraugus County)
　　　　　South Dayton Methodist Church, 1969
　　　　　one simple window

　　　Spencer (Tioga County)
　　　　　Methodist Church, 1913
　　　　　Keck's first job, *Good Samaritan*, *Guardian Angel*,
　　　　　Adoration of Shepherds (K)

　　　Summer Hill (Cayuga County)
　　　　　Summer Hill Congregational Church, 1947
　　　　　one ornamental opalescent window

　　　Sylvan Beach (Oneida County)
　　　　　St. Mary of the Lake Church, 1949
　　　　　ten mother-of-pearl opalescent windows
　　　　　church torn down, windows destroyed

Syracuse (Onondaga County)
All Saints Episcopal Church, 1926, 1931–32
St. Augustine, *St. Stephen* (W)
several windows (P)

Apostolic Christian Church, 1961
diamond windows

Assumption Cemetery, Niccola Capozzi Mausoleum, 1958
St. Anthony and Christ Child (W)

Betts Branch Library, 1963
leaded and faceted glass (W)

Blessed Sacrament Roman Catholic Church, 1930, 1951–1972
all windows in church (W), in school (B)

Dr. Charles Blum residence, 1926
Hollyhocks, *Maid of the Earth* (GB-P)

Calvary Baptist Church (United), 1915
Good Shepherd, altar; *Ruth* and *Esther*, sanctuary (K)

Calvary Evangelical United Brethren Church, 1955
diamond windows with medallions

Catholic Diocese, Rectory Chapel, 1936
St. John, *St. Patrick*, *St. Anne* (W)
windows removed to LeMoyne College Library, 1980

Mrs. H. W. Chapin residence, 1920s
many beautiful windows (W, G, B), now gone

Christ the King Roman Catholic Retreat House, 1955
Christ the King (S)

Christian Brothers Academy, 1920s
St. La Salle, *Sacred Heart* (K)

Christian Church, before 1930
Christ Blessing (K)
window rebuilt by Marjorie Miller and moved to

Congregational Church, Amber, New York, 1983, window by (W) moved to Plymouth Congregational Church

Crouse College, Syracuse University, Auditorium, 1963–1972
repair and restoration

Diocesan Residence Chapel, 1940
ornamental windows (W)

Christian Science Church, 1937
all windows made with one-inch leads

John Cummins residence, 1912
Knight in Armor on Horseback (K), window gone

Dominican Monastery of the Perpetual Rosary, 1931
ornamental, symbols (W)

Eastwood Baptist Church, 1946, 1954
Good Shepherd (W), relocated in 1954, ten symbol windows in nave (W)

Elmwood Presbyterian Church, 1917, 1931
Jesus and Woman of Samaria (Y); *Christ in Garden of Gethsemane* (K), all windows

Erwin Methodist Church, 1959
all windows (W)

Fairchild and Meech Funeral Home, before 1930
I Am the Resurrection, chapel (W)

First Baptist Church, 1956–1972
restoration of all windows designed by Norman Lindner in 1913 for Pike Studio, Rochester

First Methodist Church, 1961–1964
all windows designed by R. Shaw, painted by (S-W)

First Presbyterian Church, 1961–1964
Two-panel *Christ Blessing, Ten Commandments*, transept; *Revelation of St. John*, Keck Memorial Window (W-S-A-C)

First Universalist Church, 1915
large circular window (K), torn down

First Ward Methodist Church, 1951
all nave windows (K), see Gethsemane United Methodist

First Ward Presbyterian Church, 1916
(K)

Franciscan Convent of St. Anthony, Roman Catholic,
1949–1950
all windows in convent chapel (W)

Franciscan Convent, Novitiate, and Mother House, 1960
Adoration of the Magi (S)

Gethsemane United Methodist Church, 1970
modern *Cross* window, valle de verres (W)
rebuilt *Gethsemane* window by Keck from Park Street
Methodist Church at time of merger

Dr. Hommel residence, 1931
stair hall window (W)

Hospital of the Good Shepherd Chapel, 1917
opalescent landscape (K), now office of the Dean of the
School of Education, Huntington Hall, Syracuse University

Immaculate Conception Roman Catholic Cathedral, 1967
baptistry windows, gold leaf (Hans Brand); doors, *Shield of
Bishop*, *Holy Eucharist*, *Bust of Christ* (W)

Jesuit Provincial House, LeMoyne College, 1966
Rene Goupil, *Isaac Jogues*, *Kateri Tekakwitha*, *John
Lelande*, North American martyrs (W-A)

Lafayette Avenue Methodist Church, 1951
Christ and Evangelists (W)

Loretto Rest, 1925
ornamental painted antique glass window (W)

NEW YORK—Syracuse (*cont.*)

Most Holy Rosary Roman Catholic Church, 1930s, 1951
St. Joseph's Chapel and figure windows (P), circular
window (P) moved to new church convent

North Presbyterian Church, 1930s, 1958
opalescent with chalice (L-K); *Consider the Lilies of the
Field* opalescent (W)

O'Donnell Residence, 1926
Greek maidens in oval lozenges (GB)

Our Lady of Lourdes Roman Catholic Rectory, 1957, 1969

Our Lady of Peace Roman Catholic Church, 1961–1963
windows by Shaw, destroyed by fire

Our Lady of Pompei Roman Catholic Church, 1945–1952
clerestory and nave; *Crucifixion* after Guido Reni; *Christ
the King, St. Peter, St. Paul, St. Dominic, St. Catherine of
Siena, Blessed Virgin and Child* (W)

Our Lady of Pompei Roman Catholic School, 1965
many leaded, faceted windows (W)

Our Lady of Solace Roman Catholic Church, 1937, 1954–
1956
all windows (W)

Park Central Presbyterian Church, 1967
restoration of all windows for addition, clear leaded glass in
narthex

Pilgrim Holiness Church, 1963
cross in small circular window

Plymouth Congregational Church, 1972
restoration, diamond windows

Protestant Center Chapel, 1967
all windows, modern designs (W)

Miss E. F. Ryan residence, 1951
landscapes and painted heads (W)

Rockefeller Memorial Methodist Church, 1942
Eight opalescent, one emblem, original opalescent windows
by Keck still in old church

Sacred Heart Polish Catholic Church, 1965
Presentation, Christ in Temple, Baptism of Christ, baptistry
(A)

St. Andrew the Apostle Roman Catholic Church, 1954–
1959, 1963, all windows (W)

St. Ann's Roman Catholic Convent, 1961
Crucifixion, Resurrection, St. Joseph, Blessed Mother,
symbols (W)

St. Anthony's Roman Catholic Church, 1916–1917
guardian angels (K, P, L-K)

St. Brigid and St. Joseph Roman Catholic Church, 1957–
1971 all windows: *Christ the King, St. Mary Magdelene, St.
Theresa, Mary and Child, St. Pius X, St. Anthony with
Child, St. Anne with Child, St. John, St. Lucy, St. Patrick,
Bust of St. Peter, Bust of St. Paul*, nave: baptistry, chapel,
sacristy, and large front windows (W-W, S)

St. Daniel's Roman Catholic Church, 1954
*Sacred Heart of Jesus, Immaculate Heart of Mary, St.
Daniel, St. Joseph* (W), church torn down, windows moved
to new church and installed by another firm

St. James Roman Catholic Church, 1943, 1960–62, 1972
Nativity, Resurrection, etc., convent chapel and balcony
windows (W), all other windows (S)

St. John the Baptist Apostolic Armenian Church, 1971,
1982
Cross and Grapes, Mountains and Church, special
Armenian scenes (W)

St. John the Baptist Convent, 1949
Christ with Chalice, three ornamental windows (W)

St. John the Baptist Roman Catholic Church, 1949
grisaille pattern, *Passions of Christ*, symbols; circular
window with symbols in north transept (W)

St. John the Baptist Ukrainian Church Convent, 1963
four windows, *Cross* and three emblems (W)

St. John's Lutheran Church, n.d.
all Keck windows, torn down

St. Joseph's Hospital Chapel, 1958–1960
Christ Healing Sick, *Nativity*, eight figure groups,
four rear windows, transom, vestibule (W-S)

St. Joseph's Roman Catholic Church, 1955
windows made in 1880's redesigned by (W) installed in
clerestory and west transept windows
windows moved to Blessed Sacrament

St. Mark's Episcopal Church, 1915, 1966
Lamb of God (K), door light with cross (W)

St. Mary's Cemetery Chapel, before 1930
two ornamental windows (K)

St. Mary's Cemetery, Tassic Mausoleum, 1936
St. John the Evangelist (W)

St. Michael's Roman Catholic Church, 1930, 1950–1963
all windows: *St. Michael* (JB-K), for rectory; *St. Michael, St.
Patrick, St. Anne and Mary, Pius X*, altar (S); sacristy;
Baptism of Christ, Christ and Nicodemus, baptistry (W);
Nativity, Crucifix, Descent from Cross, Resurrection, large
front window (W); *Sacred Heart, St. John, St. Bridget, St.
Jude*, nave (W); *St. Rose of Lima, St. Columcille* (W-A)

St. Patrick's Roman Catholic Church, 1954
*Christ the King, Our Lady of Rosary, Last Supper,
Crucifixion*, ornamental windows with emblems, transoms
(W); rose window, altar destroyed by fire, altar windows
saved, restored by another firm

St. Paul's Armenian Church, 1961
Baptism of Christ, baptistry (S)

St. Paul's Episcopal Cathedral, 1926, 1954
Christ and the Rich Young Man (L-P), *U.S. Military Academy Coat of Arms* circle (K); extensive restoration work

St. Paul's Evangelical Lutheran Church, 1927, 1946
Resurrection, Christ in Gethsemane (P-K), *Nativity* (W)

St. Paul's Methodist Church, 1942, 1945
in old church on West Seneca turnpike
St. Paul, Good Shepherd, Light of the World (W)

St. Peter's Lutheran Church, before 1930
all windows by Keck, church gone

St. Peter and Paul Russian Orthodox Church, 1946, 1966
St. Andrew, Three Marys at the Tomb (W); ten figure windows: *Empty Tomb, Resurrection*, eight saints (W-A)

St. Stephen's Roman Catholic Church, before 1930, 1969
early windows by Keck, sixteen emblem windows (W)

St. Vincent de Paul Church, 1957
large transoms (W), Keck Studio remodeled over 100 windows after big fire

Seventh Day Adventist Church, 1969
large mosaic ornamental window (W)

South Presbyterian Church, before 1930, 1955
opalescent ornamentals (K), door windows (W)

Split Rock Mission Church, 1936
St. Peter (W-K)

Taunton Community Church, 1940
diamond windows with emblems (W)

NEW YORK—Syracuse (*cont.*)
Temple Beth-El, 1965
Ten Commandments in Hebrew (W)

Temple Society of Concord, 1965
Tree of Life (W)

Temple Adath Yeshurun, n.d.
early Keck windows reinstalled by another firm

Transfiguration Roman Catholic Church, 1956–1963
Ascension, Crowning of Blessed Virgin, altar; *St. Stanislaus,
St. John Cantius, Flight into Egypt, Christ and Nicodemus,
Angel and Trumpet, Finding in Temple, Christ Carrying
Cross, Crucifixion, Descent from Cross, Burial of Christ*
(W-W, S, Heim)

Trinity Episcopal Church, 1948–1968
*St. Peter, St. Andrew; Daniel, Ezekial; Isaiah, Jeremiah;
James, Philip; Obadiah, Amos; Jonah, Micah; St. Thomas,
St. Bartholomew; Nahum, Habakkuk; St. Michael, St. Uriel*
(P, W-W, A)

Trinity Lutheran Church, 1951
Luther (W)

Trinity Roman Catholic Church, before 1930
three emblems, transom (W)

University Methodist Church, 1963
inscriptions, door lights, diamond windows (W)

West Genesee Methodist Church, 1955–1960
Nativity, Easter Morn, from originals by Worden (S);
Come Unto Me, balcony window (S)

Westminster Presbyterian Church, before 1930
Easter Morn opalescent (K), church gone, window removed
to another site

Woodlawn Cemetery Mausoleum, 1940s
Fra Angelico Angel (W)

Zion Lutheran Church, before 1930
Christ on Road to Emmaus, Good Shepherd, Christ at
Home of Mary and Martha, Christ Carrying Cross (K, Y-K),
church gone

Taberg (Oneida County)
Methodist Episcopal Church, 1932
ten windows, church burned down

Troy (Rensselaer County)
Disciples of Christ Church, n.d.
closed

First Presbyterian Church, 1918, 1952–1953
Christ in Garden of Gethsemane (W), war memorial (L), *St.*
Michael (K), *Ruth and Naomi* (W)

Sacred Heart Roman Catholic Rectory, 1933
four windows

Westminster Presbyterian Church, 1926–1947
Christ in Garden of Gethsemane (W), *Nativity* (Renner-W),
Three Marys at Tomb (P), *Come Unto Me* (GB); *Lost Sheep* (W)

Tupper Lake (Franklin County)
St. Alphonsus Roman Catholic Church, 1943–1944
all windows (W)

Unadilla (Otsego County)
First Presbyterian Church, 1957–1959
twelve windows with emblems, doors, cross design

Utica (Oneida County)
Bagg Square Park Building, 1933
leaded glass

Calvary Episcopal Church, before 1930
diamond windows

NEW YORK—Utica (*cont.*)

Congregation Tiferth Zvi, 1950
twelve windows, emblems

John L. Matt Funeral Home, 1961

Moriah Presbyterian Church, 1968
cross (A)

Our Lady of Lourdes Roman Catholic Church Convent, 1959
vestibule, symbols

E. J. Quinn, undertaker, 1944
two ornamental windows

St. Agnes Roman Catholic Church and Convent, 1945–1948
rose window, ten nave windows, symbols, seven convent windows (W)

St. Francis de Sales Roman Catholic Church Convent, 1959
five emblem windows (W)

St. John's Roman Catholic Church, before 1920
Immaculate Conception circular window (Y-K)

St. Joseph's Roman Catholic Church, 1963
bust of *St. Joseph*

St. Louis Gonzaga Catholic Church, 1936
Romanesque rose, all windows

St. Mary of Mount Carmel Roman Catholic Church, 1946
Fra Angelico Angels: seven windows (W-K-K); *St. Lucy* (W)

St. Peter's Catholic Church, 1935
figure windows

St. Vincent's Mission House Chapel, 1963
St. Vincent, St. Louise de Marillac, Black Madonna, St. Casimir, Mother Seton, St. Stanislaus, Bishop's Coat of Arms (W)

134

Young Men's Christian Association, 1958
three emblem windows in chapel

Van Buren (Onondaga County)
Christ Community Church, 1961
door lights

Vestal (Broome County)
Vestal Methodist Church, 1961
cross design window, faceted glass (S)

Victory (Cayuga County)
Victory Methodist Church, 1957
unleaded opalescent windows

Warrensburg (Warren County)
Episcopal Church of the Holy Cross, 1958, 1965–1966
Christ Blessing Children, Ascension, Annunciation, Resurrection, nave (W-S-S); *Crucifixion, Christ the King,* sanctuary (S); *Baptism, Christ in Workshop, Pentecost, Boy Christ in Temple* (W-A)

Watertown (Jefferson County)
Congregation Degel Israel, 1954–1966
all windows, *Star of David, Torah, Sabbath, 24th Psalm,* etc. (W)

Episcopal Church of the Redeemer, 1969–1972
Light of the World, St. Matthew, St. John (W)

First Methodist Church, 1958
Christ in Garden of Gethsemane circular window (W-S)

St. Anthony's Roman Catholic Church, 1934–1942
Sacred Heart of Jesus, Mary, St. Anthony, St. Cecilia, Annunciation, St. Aloysius, St. Veronica's Napkin, Crucifixion and *Our Lady of Sorrows, Holy Family, Sacred Jesus; St. Stephen Bishop, Our Lady of Mt. Carmel* (W)

NEW YORK (*cont.*)

    Watervliet (Albany County)

        Church (Reverend Cirino), 1925–1927
        Blessed Mother and Child, St. Rocco, emblems, *St. Theresa*, etc. (P)

    Weedsport (Cayuga County)

        First Presbyterian Church, 1941–1958
        Christ Blessing Children (Reiger-K); *Gethsemane* (SW); *St. Peter, Light of the World* (W-S)

        Weedsport Methodist Church, 1956
        Good Shepherd (W)

    West Bangor (Franklin County)

        St. Edward's Roman Catholic Church, 1963–1964
        emblem windows

    West Stockholm (St. Lawrence County)

        Methodist Church, 1967–1968
        twelve windows with symbols (W-A)

    Westport (Essex County)

        St. Philip's Roman Catholic Church, 1944
        all windows (W)

    Whitesboro (Oneida County)

        St. Anne's Roman Catholic Church, 1969–1970
        St. Anne and Blessed Mother (W)

    Willard (Seneca County)

        Christ Episcopal Church, 1962–1963, 1966
        Jesus Teacher, Jesus Healer, Baptism of Christ, Christ and Nicodemus (W)

    Williamson (Wayne County)

        Presbyterian Church, 1946–1947
        one glass mosaic panel

Williamstown (Oswego County)
    St. Patrick's, 1926
    altar window

Woodgate (Oneida County)
    Round Lake Masonic Home, 1934
    Christ Blessing Children (W)

NORTH CAROLINA
    Black Mountain
        St. James Episcopal Church, 1942–1943
        St. James (W-K), three-panel altar window

    Charlotte
        St. Patrick's Roman Catholic Church, 1939
        *St. Patrick Preaching, Annunciation, Gethsemane, Rich
        Young Man, Healing Blind Man, Ascension, Crucifixion,
        Boy Christ in Temple, Mary Magdelene, Washing Christ's
        Feet, Blessing Children* (W)

    Cooleemee
        Church of the Good Shepherd, 1935, 1946–47, 1954
        Christ Come Unto Me, four windows with emblems (W)

    Elizabeth City
        Cann Memorial Presbyterian Church, 1944
        one rose window (W)

    Fayetteville
        St. James' Lutheran Church, 1943
        eight windows with life of Christ (W)

    Fletcher
        Calvary Episcopal Church, 1946–1966
        all windows (W)

NORTH CAROLINA (*cont.*)
Fort Bragg
82nd Airborne Division Chapel, 1959
St. Michael (S)

Glen Alpine
Glen Alpine Methodist Church, 1945–1946
Christ Come Unto Me (W)

Marion
First Methodist Church, 1960–1961
Christ the Good Shepherd (W-S)

Parkton
Southern Presbyterian Church, 1948
one ornamenal window

Raleigh
Sacred Heart Roman Catholic Cathedral, 1941
all windows in church (W)

Salisbury
Sacred Heart Roman Catholic Church, 1942–1943
St. Peter, St. Benedict, St. Patrick, St. Anthony, St. Gregory Great, Sacred Heart of Jesus, Sacred Heart of Mary, St. Theresa, St. Leo, St. Paul, St. John (W, Renner-W), *Sisters of Mercy* circular window (W)

Smithfield
Centenary Methodist Church, 1949–1950
opalescent and cathedral glass windows with emblems in antique glass (W)

First Baptist Church, 1951–1953
twelve ornamental windows in church, eighteen in chapel, all opalescent and antique glass windows with emblems (W)

Wake Forest
Spring Street Presbyterian Church, 1949
glass cut to size for sixteen windows, no leading involved

NORTH DAKOTA
Alamo
Trinity Lutheran Church, 1947–1949
three windows, large pieces of glass set in wood

Bathgate
Bathgate Presbyterian Church, 1959
Christ Blessing Children, Christ in Gethsemane (W-S)

Makoti
Church, 1943
two opalescent windows

Parshall
First Lutheran Church, 1943–1945
nine opalescent windows with symbols (W)

Sanish
Norwegian Lutheran Church, 1946
one ornamental window

Sanish English Lutheran Church, 1948–1949
opalescent window

OHIO
Bowling Green
First Presbyterian Church, 1938
twenty-four large ornate windows, all with scenes of the
Bible in medallions. Signing of the contract was a life-saver
for the Keck Studio. Most major studios in the U.S. were
bidding for it.

North Baltimore
Methodist Church, 1941
one cross window, sixteen large windows

OHIO (*cont.*)
    Van Wert

        First Presbyterian Church, 1939–1956
        most windows, seven-lancet balcony window: *Book of Revelations; Christ Blessing Children*, Sunday school (W). Stanley Worden believes this was the largest and finest set of windows the studio ever made.

PENNSYLVANIA
    Altoona

        St. George's Syrian Orthodox Church, 1948
        five emblem windows (W)

    Blossburg

        St. Luke's Church, 1945–1952
        St. Cecilia, St. Luke, St. Peter, Christ the King (W)

    Canton

        Church of Christ, 1960
        Christ in Gethsemane (S)

    DuBois

        First Presbyterian Church, 1959
        Lamb of God, ornamental (W)

    New Hope

        New Hope Methodist Church, 1934
        three memorial windows

    Sayre

        Episcopal Church of the Redeemer, 1940–1963
        Matthew, Mark, Luke, and John; Christ the King, in chancel; *Blessing Children, Washing Apostles' Feet* (W)

        First Presbyterian Church, 1956–1967
        Last Supper, Blessing Children, Good Shepherd; sunburst (½ circle), clerestory, ornamental (W, S-S)

Scranton
>Saints Peter and Paul Roman Catholic Church, 1942
>*St. Peter, St. Paul* (W), altar windows

Summit Hill
>Mausoleum, 1965
>small window, cross design (W)

Towanda
>Christ Church, 1916

Troy
>St. Paul's Episcopal Church, 1946
>*Nativity* (W)

Wayne
>St. Mary's Rectory, 1941
>four small windows with symbols (W)

RHODE ISLAND
>Providence
>>Hassenfeld Residence, 1930s
>>library window, *Coat of Arms*

>>Temple Beth-Israel, 1933–1937

>>Temple Emanu-El, 1934, 1953
>>twenty-six large windows, history of Jewish faith (W), seven
>>windows with symbols of Psalms, one circle window

SOUTH CAROLINA
>Anderson
>>Salem Presbyterian Church, 1954
>>ornamental circular window with chalice (W)

>Hartsville
>>Kelleytown Baptist Church, 1944–1950
>>ornamental window, stock design #35

TENNESSEE
>Nashville
>>Mrs. R. S. Clark, circa 1925
>>*David, Moses* (JB)

TEXAS
>Galveston
>>Trinity Episcopal Church, 1949–1959
>>*Nativity, Boy Christ in Temple* (W)

UTAH
>Provo
>>St. Mary's Episcopal Church, 1965
>>*St. John, St. Mary and Child* (W-A)

VERMONT
>Brandon
>>Wesleyan Methodist Church, 1938
>>nave; seven emblems; *Light of the World* circular (W)

>Shelburne
>>Methodist Episcopal Church, 1937
>>large ornamental opalescent window (W-K)

VIRGINIA
>Blackstone
>>Crenshaw Methodist Church, 1949–1969
>>all windows: *Good Shepherd, Light of the World*, rose
>>window, *Christ with Ten Commandments, Nativity,*
>>*Resurrection*, symbols of *Twelve Apostles*, balcony (W)

Brandy
        Christ Church, 1936–1937
        Baptism of Christ, Christ Blessing Children, Good Shepherd
        (W), church destroyed by fire

Frederick Hall
        Protestant Church, circa 1942
        Good Shepherd (W)

Fredericksburg
        Mary Washington Hospital, 1963–1964
        eight small glass panels, modern design

Glade Spring
        Glade Spring Presbyterian Church, 1951
        Good Shepherd (K)

Kenbridge
        Kenbridge Methodist Church, 1943–1944
        all opalescent windows

Richmond
        Decatur Street Methodist Church, 1960
        Christ in Gethsemane circle window (W)

        Forest Hill Presbyterian Church, 1947
        ornamental circle window (W)

        St. Philip's Episcopal Church, 1949–1950
        opalescent window, design #2; *St. Philip* (W)

Roanoke
        Second Presbyterian Church, 1941, 1951–1959
        all windows: narthex five-panel (W-S); rose window (W);
        ornamental, chapel (W); figure groups: *Sower, Good
        Samaritan, Lost Sheep, Light of the World, Well Done
        Good and Faithful Servant, Rich Young Man, Christ
        Blessing, Good Shepherd, Healing Paralytic, Behold the
        Lilies, Christ and Nicodemus, Healing Servant and*

VIRGINIA—Roanoke (*cont.*)
  Centurion, Widow's Mite, Blessing Loaves and Fishes, Jesus Walking on Water, Marriage and Feast at Cana, Stilling Tempest, Miraculous Draft of Fishes, Precious Ointment, Raising Lazarus (W)

  Washington
  Trinity Episcopal Church, 1936
  six medallion figure windows, three vestibule windows, one circular window (W)

WEST VIRGINIA
  Wellsburgh
  Methodist Episcopal Church, 1938
  Christ in Gethsemane, after Hoffman (painted by W)

WISCONSIN
  Prairie du Sac
  Evangelical and Reformed Church, 1947
  nine ornamental windows with emblems (W)

WYOMING
  Green River
  St. John's Episcopal Church, 1945
  St. John circle window (W)

  Lander
  Episcopal Church, 1949
  Christ and Doubting Thomas (W)

Exhibition Catalogue List

he first comprehensive exhibition of the work of the Henry Keck Stained Glass Studio was organized by Cleota Reed for IDEA, Inc., and held at the Onondaga Historical Association in Syracuse, New York, from October 15, 1983, to February 1, 1984. It included historic photographs, original works of art—watercolors, cartoons, and panels of stained glass loaned from several sources—tools of the stained glass artist and artisan, and a thirty-minute videotape production, "Reflections of a Stained Glass Artist: Stanley Worden and the Keck Studio." The exhibition was mounted and framed by the Studio Gallery, Syracuse, and the Gallery Association of New York. A record of the exhibition follows.

INTRODUCTION

1. *Romance; Wine, Women & Song; Dance; Music; The Chase; Your Health; Feast; Hope.* Eight stained glass windows for rathskeller in former M. C. Eaton Residence, Norwich, New York. Designed and painted by Stanley Worden. 1933. *Courtesy: Norwich Jewish Center.*

2. *Dance.* Full scale cartoon. Ink on paper, 19 x 17½". Artist: Stanley Worden. 1933. *Keck Archives.*

3. *Romance; Wine, Women & Song; Dance; Music.* Watercolor, 1½ x 15", for Eaton rathskeller windows. Artist: Stanley Worden. 1933. *Keck Archives.*

4. *The Revelation of St. John.* Watercolor, 22¼ x 16⅝", for stained glass window. Executed by artists and craftsmen of the Keck Studio as a memorial to Henry and Myra Keck and their daughter, Elisabeth. 1964. First Presbyterian Church, Syracuse, New York. *Private collection.*

5-25.   Series of documentary photographs taken between 1928 and 1967 showing artists and craftsmen of the Keck Studio making stained glass windows. Photos by Dick Bandy, Stanley Worden, and others, unknown. *Keck Archives.*

THE EARLY YEARS: Changing Styles and Traditions, 1913–1929

26.   *Ascension.* Watercolor, 13¾ x 6″. Design for opalescent window. Artist: Charles Young. Before 1920. *Private collection.*

27.   *Christ in the Garden of Gethsemane* after Heinrich Hoffman. Watercolor, 13¼ x 5⅜″. Design for opalescent window. Artist: Henry Keck. Before 1920. *Keck Archives.*

28.   *Christ Blessing.* Watercolor, 20¾ x 16½″. Design for three-panel opalescent window. Artist: Henry Keck. Before 1920. *Keck Archives.*

29.   *Grape Arbor.* Watercolor, 24 x 24″. One-half inch scale design for retractable opalescent glass skylight for Archmere, residence of John Jacob Raskob, now Archmere Academy, Claymont, Delaware. Artist: Henry Keck. 1917. *Private collection.*

30.   Two views of "The Patio" of Archmere showing *Grape Arbor* skylight as it appears in 1983. *Photo: Cleota Reed.*

31.   *Maid of the Earth.* Charcoal and ink, 109 x 36″. Full scale cartoon for center panel of antique glass window for former Dr. Blum residence, Syracuse. Artists: Henry Keck and Bernhardt. 1926. *Keck Archives.*

32.   *Maid of the Earth.* Three-panel stained glass window in Syracuse residence. *Photo: Courtney Frisse. 1982*

33.   *Landscape.* Watercolor, 5¼ x 9″. Design for five-lancet opalescent window for chapel of the Hospital of the Good Shepherd, now Huntington Hall, Syracuse University. Artist: Henry Keck. 1917. *Private collection.*

34.   *Landscape.* Watercolor. 5 x 9″. Design for five-lancet opalescent window. Artist: Henry Keck. c. 1915. Location unknown. *Private collection.*

35.   Landscape window in Huntington Hall, Syracuse University. *Photo: Courtney Frisse. 1983.*

36.   *Dogwood.* Watercolor, 5⅝ x 3½″. Design for stained glass window for Syracuse residence. Artist: Henry Keck. 1930. *Keck Archives.*

37. *Knowledge*. Watercolor, 5¾ x 5". Design for antique stained glass window for Hassenfeld residence, Providence, Rhode Island. Artist: Stanley Worden. 1930s. *Keck Archives.*

38. *Nursery Rhymes*. Watercolor, four subjects, 1¾ x 2½" each. Designs for stained glass windows for child's room. Artist: Henry Keck. Window location unknown. 1920s. *Private collection.*

39. *Knight*. Watercolor, 4¾ x 2⅜". Design for stained glass window for former Dr. Harding residence, Jordan, New York. Artist: Stanley Worden. 1935. *Keck Archives.*

40. *Knight*. Stained glass panel, 24½ x 13½". Designed and painted by Stanley Worden. 1935. *Keck Archives.*

41. *Library motifs*. Watercolor, 2⅜ x 2". Designs for stained glass medallions. Artist: Stanley Worden. 1929. *Private collection.*

42. *Music*. Watercolor, 4 x 1". Design for stained glass medallion for music room of private residence. Artist: Henry Keck. 1929. *Private collection.*

43. *Appetite and Health*. Watercolor, 2¾ x 5⅞". Design for stained glass window for Zuber residence, Norwich, New York. Artist: Stanley Worden. 1930s. *Keck Archives.*

44. *The Three Kings*. Sepia and black ink, 8 x 6⅝". Design for two-panel neo-Gothic antique stained glass window. Artist: Norman Lindner. c. 1920. *Private collection.*

45. *Life of Christ*. Watercolor, 19½ x 10½". Design for neo-Gothic antique stained glass window. Artist: Stanley Worden. 1929. *Keck Archives.*

46. *St. Cecilia*. Watercolor, 4¼" diameter. Design for opalescent, enameled, plated window for St. Mary's Roman Catholic Church, Mexico, New York. Artist: Henry Keck. 1915. *Private collection.*

47. *St. Cecilia*. Stained, painted, and plated window for St. Mary's Church, Mexico, New York, made by Henry Keck. 1930s. *Photo: Courtney Frisse. 1982.*

48. *Three Scenes from the Life of Christ*. Watercolor, 14 x 13". Design for three-panel antique glass window for St. Joseph's Roman Catholic Church, Dannemora, New York. Artist: Stanley Worden. 1931. *Keck Archives.*

49. Opalescent, plated neo-Gothic ornamental stained glass panel, 23 x 42". Artist: Henry Keck. Before 1910. *Keck Archives.*

50. *Christ the King*. Stained glass panel. 23½ x 18¼". Designed and painted by Henry Keck to use in studio as display of typical early style. c. 1915. *Keck Archives.*

51. *St. John*. Stained glass panel, 21½ x 15″. Designed and painted by Henry Keck as display piece for studio showroom. c. 1915. *Keck Archives.*

52. *Art*. Stained glass panel. 40½ x 21″. Designed and painted by Henry Keck for use as a doorlight in Keck Studio. 1925. *Private collection.*

53. *Music*. Stained glass panel. 40½ x 21″. Designed and painted by Henry Keck for use as a doorlight in Keck Studio. 1925. *Private collection.*

THE MIDDLE YEARS: 1929–1956

54. *St. Theresa and St. Patrick*. Watercolor, 10¾ x 6⅜″. Design for two-panel neo-Gothic antique stained glass window for Church of the Immaculate Conception, Pompey, New York. Artist: *Stanley Worden.*

55. *St. Elizabeth: Charity & Consecration*. Watercolor, 12¾ x 6¼″. Design for two panel Neo-Gothic antique stained glass window for St. Joseph's Roman Catholic Church, Middletown, New York. Artist: Stanley Worden. 1935. *Keck Archives.*

56. *St. Anne*. Full scale cartoon, 57½ x 22″, for one of four stained glass windows for Catholic Diocese Rectory Chapel, Syracuse, New York. Artist: Stanley Worden. 1936. Windows moved to LeMoyne College Library in 1980. *Keck Archives.*

57. *St. Patrick*. Antique stained glass panel, 29 x 18″. Designed and painted by Stanley Worden. Replica of section of window for Catholic Diocese Rectory Chapel. *Keck Archives.*

58. *Book of Revelations*. Watercolor, 21 x 10¼″. Design for five lancet neo-Gothic antique stained glass window for First Presbyterian Church, Van Wert, Ohio. Artist: Stanley Worden. 1939. *Keck Archives.*

59. *Nativity*. Watercolor, 14 x 14½″. Design for seven-lancet neo-Gothic antique stained glass window for Gobin Memorial Methodist Church, DePauw University, Greencastle, Indiana. Artist: Stanley Worden. 1947. *Keck Archives.*

60. *Christ and the Evangelists*. Watercolor, 21½ x 15″. Design for neo-Gothic antique stained glass window for Lafayette Methodist Church, Syracuse, New York. Artist: Stanley Worden. 1951. *Keck Archives.*

61. *Scenes from the Life of Christ*. Watercolor, 23½ x 16⅝″. Design for three-panel stained glass window with circle tops. Artist: Stanley Worden. 1950. Not executed. *Keck Archives.*

NEW YORK STATE SUBJECTS

62. *Francis Asbury, Methodist Circuit Rider.* Watercolor, 10½ x 5″. Design for stained glass window for Methodist Church, Sidney, New York. Artist: Stanley Worden. 1933. *Keck Archives.*

63. *St. Isaac Jogues.* Watercolor, 8 x 2¾″. Design for figure window for St. Mary's Roman Catholic Church, Mexico, New York. Artist: Stanley Worden. 1944. *Keck Archives.*

64. *Kateri Tekakwitha.* Charcoal and ink, full-scale cartoon, 64 x 28″. Design for stained glass window for Catholic Church of the Resurrection, Germantown, New York. Artist: Stanley Worden. 1933. *Keck Archives.*

65. *Good Shepherd.* Watercolor, 8¼ x 11″. Design for three-panel stained glass window for St. Eustace Episcopal Church, Lake Placid, New York. Artist: Ernest Ashcroft. 1964. *Keck Archives.*

66. *Immaculate Conception.* Watercolor, 18¾ x 11¾″. Design for antique stained glass window for altar of St. Mary's Roman Catholic Church, Amsterdam, New York. Artist: Stanley Worden. 1942. *Keck Archives.*

67. *Seal of State of New York, Peter Minuit and DeWitt Clinton.* Full-scale cartoons for sections of enameled, opalescent window, 10′ x 6′9″, for Assembly Chamber anteroom, New York State Capitol, Albany. Artist: David Lithgow. 1950. *Keck Archives.*

68. Stained glass window in State Capitol. *Photo: Courtney Frisse.*

WAR MEMORIALS

69. *St. Michael.* Sepia and ink, 9¼ x 4⅝″. Design for stained glass World War I memorial window for First Presbyterian Church, Troy, New York. Artist: Norman Lindner. 1918. *Private collection.*

70. *Mass on World War I Battlefield.* Watercolor, 3½ x 3½″. Design for stained glass World War I memorial window for St. Joseph's Roman Catholic Church, Middletown, New York. Artist: Stanley Worden. 1932. *Keck Archives.*

71. *St. Michael: Prince of the Church Militant.* Watercolor, 9½ x 3″. Design for antique stained glass window for World War II memorial. Not executed. Artist: Stanley Worden. 1946. *Keck Archives.*

72. *St. Michael.* Watercolor, 5 x 2⅝″. Design for stained glass World War II memorial window for St. Michael's Church, Onondaga Hill, Syracuse, New York. Artist: Ronald Shaw. 1956. *Keck Archives.*

73. *The Spirit of Freedom.* Watercolor, 4¼ x 3½". Design for World War II memorial window for Canastota, New York, High School. Artist: Stanley Worden. 1944. *Keck Archives.*

74. *St. Michael.* Watercolor, 15 x 8". Design for antique stained glass World War II memorial window for the Episcopal Church of the Ascension, Rochester, New York. Artist: Stanley Worden. 1946. *Keck Archives.*

75. *St. Michael* window in Church of the Ascension, Rochester, New York (no. 74). *Photo: Courtney Frisse.*

76. *St. Michael and the Twelve Virtues.* Watercolor, 12" diameter. Design for stained glass World War II memorial rose window for First Presbyterian and Trinity Church, South Orange, New Jersey. Artist: Stanley Worden. 1947-48. *Keck Archives.*

77. *St. Michael.* Watercolor, 16 x 12¼". Design for stained glass World War II memorial window for the 82nd Airborne Chapel, Fort Bragg, North Carolina. Artist: Ronald Shaw. 1959. *Keck Archives.*

78. *Liberty.* Watercolor, 16 x 9½". Design for antique stained glass World War II memorial window for St. Mary's Roman Catholic Church, Amsterdam, New York. Artist: Stanley Worden. 1945. *Keck Archives.*

79. *Liberty.* West transept window for St. Mary's Church, Amsterdam, New York (no. 78). *Photo: Courtney Frisse.*

LATER SACRED SUBJECTS: Christian and Jewish

80. *The Annunciation.* Watercolor, 14¼ x 3½". Design for stained glass window for St. Francis Xavier Roman Catholic Church, Marcellus, New York. Artist: Stanley Worden. 1945. *Keck Archives.*

81. *Crossing the Bar.* Watercolor, 6 x 3½". Design for stained glass window illustrating the poem by Tennyson, in Timme mausoleum, Cold Spring on Hudson, New York. Artist: Stanley Worden. 1940s. *Keck Archives.*

82. *Crucifixion.* Watercolor, 13½ x 5¼". Design for one of nave windows illustrating the life of Christ for Church of the Transfiguration, Syracuse, New York. Artist: Stanley Worden. 1956. *Keck Archives.*

83. *Baptism of Christ; Holy Mother; Christ and Nicodemus.* Three watercolors, 4½ x 2¼" each. Design for baptistry windows for St. Mary's Church, Amsterdam, New York. Artist: Stanley Worden. 1948. *Keck Archives.*

84. Full-scale cartoons, 58 x 30″ each, for baptistry windows (no. 83) for St. Mary's Church, Amsterdam, New York. Artist: Stanley Worden. 1948. *Keck Archives.*

85. *Good Shepherd.* Stained glass window, 34½ x 22″ lozenge, used by Henry Keck as demonstration model. Painted and leaded up after his death by Stanley Worden. *Private collection.*

86. *Christ and the Apostles.* Watercolor, 9″ diameter. Design for antique stained glass rose window for the Franciscan Convent Chapel, Syracuse, New York. Artist: Stanley Worden. 1950. *Keck Archives.*

87. *Christ the King.* Watercolor, 15½ x 12½″. Design for three-panel stained glass window for chancel of St. Paul's Episcopal Church, Endicott, New York. Artist: Stanley Worden. 1956. *Keck Archives.*

88. *Tree of Life.* Watercolor, 4⅛ x 5½″. Design for stained glass window for Temple Concord, Syracuse, New York. Artist: Ernest Ashcroft. 1965. *Keck Archives.*

89. *Mercy.* Watercolor, 7¼ x 3½″. Design for stained glass window for Congregation Ahwoth Chesid, Jacksonville, Florida. Artist: Stanley Worden, 1956. *Keck Archives.*

90. *History of Jewish Faith.* Watercolor, 19 x 4″. Master design for 14 school windows for Temple Emanu-El, Providence, Rhode Island. Artist: Stanley Worden. 1953. *Keck Archives.*

91. *Justice.* Watercolor, 27¼ x 4″. Design for synagogue window in Hartford, Connecticut. Artist: Henry Keck. circa 1926. *Keck Archives.*

92. *History of Jewish Faith.* Watercolor for fourteen figure panels, 5 x 2½″ each, for Temple Emanu-El, Providence, Rhode Island (no. 90A). Artist: Stanley Worden. 1953. *Keck Archives.*

93. *Jewish Immigrants Arrive in New York.* Ink and watercolor, 60 x 32″. Full-scale cartoon for figure window for Temple Emanu-El (no. 90A), Providence, Rhode Island. Artist: Stanley Worden. 1953. *Keck Archives.*

TOWARD A MODERN IDIOM, 1956–1974

94. *Our Lady of Solace.* Watercolor, 25½ x 13″. Design for stained glass window for Our Lady of Solace Roman Catholic Church, Syracuse, New York. Artist: Stanley Worden. 1954. *Keck Archives.*

95. *Come Unto Me.* Watercolor, 12¾ x 12″. Design for three-panel stained glass window for West Genesee Street Methodist Church, Syracuse, New York. Artist: Ronald Shaw. 1955–1960. *Keck Archives.*

96. *Holy Trinity.* Watercolor, 21½ x 14¼″. Design for stained glass window. Artist: Ronald Shaw. 1960. Not executed. *Keck Archives.*

97. *Christmas Morn.* Watercolor, 3⅝″ diameter. Design for circular stained glass window for West Genesee Methodist Church, Syracuse, New York. Artist: Ronald Shaw. 1960. *Keck Archives.*

98. *Easter Morn.* Companion window for no. 97. *Keck Archives.*

99. *Christmas Morn.* Ink on paper, 48″ square. Full-scale cartoon for no. 97. *Keck Archives.*

100. *Nativity.* Stained glass panel, 20⅝ x 14¾″, used as sample at Keck Studio. Artist: Ronald Shaw. 1960. *Keck Archives.*

Index

HENRY KECK STAINED GLASS STUDIO, 1913–1974

was composed in 11-point Mergenthaler Sabon on a Linotron 202 and leaded 2 points,
with display type in Caslon Open, by Dix Type, Inc.,
and chapter opening Cloister Initials;
4-color insert printed by sheet-fed offset on 70-pound, acid-free Warren Patina,
and 4-color paper covers printed by sheet-fed offset on 3–12-point Kivar
by Frank A. West Company, Inc.;
text printed in 2 colors by sheet-fed offset on 70-pound, acid-free Warren Patina,
Smythe-sewn and bound over binder's boards in Joanna Arrestox B,
also Smythe-sewn with Kivar covers tipped on
by Maple-Vail Book Manufacturing Group, Inc.;
designed by Sara Lepper Eddy;
and published by

SYRACUSE UNIVERSITY PRESS

SYRACUSE, NEW YORK 13210